YOUR COMPANY IS GOING TO SHUT DOWN

YOUR COMPANY IS GOING TO SHUT DOWN

ABHISHEK VYAS

AMARYLLIS

AMARYLLIS

An imprint of Manjul Publishing House Pvt. Ltd.
• C-16, Sector 3, Noida, Uttar Pradesh 201 301, India
Website: www.manjulindia.com
Registered Office:
• 2nd Floor, Usha Preet Complex, 42 Malviya Nagar, Bhopal 462 003 – India
Distribution Centres
Ahmedabad, Bengaluru, Chennai, Hyderabad,
Kochi, Kolkata, Mumbai, Noida, Pune

Your Company is Going to Shut Down by Abhishek Vyas

This paperback edition first published in India in 2025

ISBN 978-93-5543-480-7

Cover image: Shutterstock

Printed and bound in India by Repro India Limited

Contents

1

Truth: Path to Clarity

———◆———

'TRUTH IS THE BASIC CONDITION FOR STARTING ANY business. Unless we stand by the truth with loyalty towards our objectives, goals and duties, we cannot achieve success.

'I cannot claim with certainty that the "truth" I have experienced in my 19-year business journey will be the same for you. The path that has been useful to me may not necessarily work for you. My truth cannot be your truth. It would be misleading to say that adopting the ideas that helped me reach where I am today will guarantee your success. Believe me, the lessons I've learned in these years, the ones that helped me build and establish my company in the market, are simply my version of the truth.

'This is the continuous experience of my life, which I have lived and adopted every day. I cannot give you the truth of this success even if I want to.'

Truth is not something that can be asked for, nor can it be distributed. Even if I were to share all the secrets behind my company's success and suggest that you could replicate them to build your own, it would still not be the truth. Even if I laid out every method in full detail, it would still look false to you. Truth cannot be spoken because it has no clear definition. It cannot be written, as it is not bound by words. In the time it takes for me to write it, to say it, and for it to reach you, it will have changed. There is a vast difference between truth and words. The moment a truth becomes a word, it changes, becomes distorted, and ceases to be the truth. So, if you are seeking a formula for success, a method to become a billionaire in a year, or principles that guarantee achievement in this book, I urge you to stop right here. In the end, you will only find disappointment. Still, I will share what I have come to know as 'truth' in my own journey to success in the hope that by understanding it, you may discover the truth in your own path.

In my journey of success, I have come to know that truth is just a hint. It can only point towards the truth following which I have achieved success. But if you consider this hint as the ultimate truth and search for success, then it will be a grave mistake. My truth can be just an indication, a direction, a principle, which can be considered as a mere understanding of success. But it will be foolish to consider this alone as the mantra for success. Truth means the experience of your life. What you discover via your experience is the truth for you. What you are ready to accept, is the truth for you.

A long time ago, there lived a Brahmin, a simple and humble man devoted to God. He wandered from place to place, reciting the Bhagwat, and accepted whatever came his way as divine will. In his contentment, he found peace.

But there's a hidden danger in being satisfied. Contentment, while seemingly virtuous, can also act as a barrier in life. It can become a silent disease, an obstacle that stops us from exploring the full potential of our existence. Life is full of mysteries, and nature has woven the earth with an exquisite fragrance of endless possibilities. This gift—the experience of these mysteries—is one of life's greatest blessings. To savour this fragrance is to be truly fortunate.

Today, humanity dreams of establishing colonies in space. Had we remained satisfied with life on Earth, would this ever have been possible? Certainly not. In truth, it is only through dissatisfaction that new opportunities arise. That's why I say, if you aspire for success in life, you must remain restless, always seeking more. Satisfaction with your current position will prevent you from discovering the hidden mysteries that life and the marketplace have to offer.

Yet, society teaches us to be satisfied. We are told to accept what we have and call it destiny. But I believe that those who speak of fate are the ones who have already surrendered to the belief that they are not capable of more. It's a sign of weakened ambition. But rather than face the truth of their own shortcomings, they take the easy route, blaming fate while justifying their complacency.

This is why I urge you—if you wish to reach your fullest potential, you must reject contentment. Do not sit idly by, relying on fate, and praying for miracles. Whether in life or business, miracles do not happen. The ones who expect miracles are often those who are satisfied with mediocrity, who believe there is nothing beyond what they have.

The Brahmin, in his simplicity, was satisfied with whatever life gave him. He accepted everything as part of God's grand design and found happiness in that. But for those of us seeking to evolve, to grow beyond our current state, satisfaction can become a trap. It is only through dissatisfaction that we push boundaries and discover the vast possibilities awaiting us.

Once, a grand Yagya was organised in the kingdom, and the king invited all the priests and pundits from far and wide. Among them was the Brahmin, who had been fortunate enough to attend the magnificent event. The Yagya was a splendid affair, culminating in lavish offerings. As dakshina, the priests and pundits were given animals— some received cows, others goats, and a few were gifted sheep.

The Brahmin was given a young Pathani horse colt, just 6 or 7 months old. Though he thanked the Lord for the gift, inwardly he felt disheartened. As he carried the colt on his shoulders, he muttered to himself, 'What use is this colt to me? If only I had received a cow, I would have milk to drink and the blessing of serving it. Now, instead of relief, I have the burden of feeding this animal when I can barely feed myself.'

With these thoughts weighing on his mind, the Brahmin hurried along, anxious to reach home before nightfall. The colt's weight was beginning to strain his shoulders, and the growing fear of the dangers that could lurk along the path added to his distress.

He had barely covered a mile or two when four thieves took notice of the Brahmin and his valuable colt. Sensing an opportunity of making quick money, they decided to trick him. They devised a plan to deceive the Brahmin and stood waiting along the road, spaced at intervals.

As the Brahmin approached the first thug, the man greeted him with a sly smile, 'Ram, Ram, Pandit ji! Why are you carrying this mule? It's not fitting for a respected Brahmin like yourself to be burdened with such a useless animal. Why not sell it to me for 10 rupees? That way, you'll be rid of the load, and you'll have some cash to spare as well.'

The Brahmin, though tired, was taken aback by the man's words, wondering why he would mistake the colt for a mule. Still, he continued on his way, unaware of the trickery unfolding ahead.

Upon hearing the thug's words, the Brahmin felt a surge of anger, but he restrained himself. 'You must be a fool to call a colt a mule. Fear God and let me be,' he said sharply, quickening his pace. The thug, undeterred, followed closely behind, mocking him. 'You're an incredible man, Maharaj ji, getting angry for no reason! I offered you a good deal—no one else would pay even two rupees for this weak mule.'

Ignoring the first thug, the Brahmin continued on his way, only to be intercepted by a second one. This one bowed respectfully and touched the Brahmin's feet, saying, 'Maharaj ji, I am truly blessed to have crossed paths with you. I've heard much about your greatness. But I must say, it troubles me to see a man of your stature carrying such a feeble donkey. What good is it to you? I'd be honoured to take it off your hands for six or seven rupees and cherish it as a token of your blessing for the rest of my life.'

This time, the Brahmin's patience wore thin. Furious, he snapped, 'You must be an irreligious fool! Are you intoxicated? How dare you call this colt a donkey? Go on your way and leave me alone!'

Frustrated but now growing uncertain, the Brahmin pressed on. His earlier conviction began to waver. Could it be that the colt was not a horse after all? Doubts started creeping in.

A little further down the road, the third thug repeated the same charade, feeding further into the Brahmin's confusion. His uncertainty now transformed into belief.

Finally, he spotted the fourth and last thug standing ahead, waiting as if anticipating his arrival. The Brahmin thought, 'Let me ask this man and clear my doubts once and for all.' Approaching the thug, he said, 'Brother, I'm deeply confused. Look at this colt—does it resemble a mule or a donkey, or is it indeed a horse's foal as I believe? On my way, I've met several people who insist it's a mule or a donkey. You seem like a reasonable man; help me settle this.'

The thug, well-prepared for this moment, laughed loudly and said, 'Maharaj ji, I respect you too much to lie. You're a man of honour, and I would hate to disagree with you, but I must swear by Lord Shiva that this is not a horse's foal. This is clearly an Arabian mule. I know this because my distant uncle, a washerman by trade, once brought a mule just like this from Arabia. I remember sitting on its back as a child at the dhobi ghat.'

Hearing this, the Brahmin felt as though the ground had shifted beneath him. He cursed the king in his mind, cursed his fate, and then hesitantly asked the thug, 'Brother, you seem knowledgeable about mules. What do you think this one is worth in the market?'

The thug glanced at the Brahmin from head to toe, raising his eyebrows as he replied, 'Only a fool would pay for such a lifeless mule. If I had to put a price on it, I wouldn't give even three rupees.'

'Would you offer two and a half rupees?' the Brahmin blurted out.

The thug laughed. 'Maharaj ji, for you, I would! But I am no businessman, just a poor labourer. I only have two rupees in my pocket. If you're willing, I'll take this burden off your shoulders.'

The Brahmin, worn down and now fully convinced, quickly agreed. Satisfied with two rupees, he handed over the colt and walked away, feeling lighter but unaware of the deception that had just unfolded.

This is why I say, on the path to success, we must change our habit of blindly believing in what we perceive as truth. We cannot achieve true understanding until we begin to see things as they really are.

Truth means understanding what *is*—an awareness that cannot be based on belief but only on comprehension. Truth is about perceiving reality as it exists. However, the dilemma we face as humans is that we have accepted truth in the form of principles, scriptures, and stories. If we truly want to get closer to the truth, we must first learn the art of dissatisfaction, which begins by letting go of blind belief.

We must start seeing things as they are, without the veil of preconceived notions.

What we often mistake as the truth of our lives—by imitating the success of others, by following their journeys, by adhering to the principles they set, and by walking the paths they've shown us—needs to be unlearned. We have to find our own path to the truth, our own path to success. Accepting someone else's formula for success may prevent you from embarking on the unique journey that leads you to your own peak.

Remember, every individual's struggle is different, and so is their understanding of life. The definitions of success and failure vary for each of us, so it's not necessary that the same truth applies to you as it does to someone else. In this business journey, we must carve our own path to success. In life, we must discover our unique truth—the one that belongs solely to us.

I have discovered many profound truths throughout my professional journey, and one of the most important is this: the past cannot be rewritten, the present cannot be escaped, and the only way to shape the future is by acting in the present. In its essence, the present is the only truth. What has passed is simply memory, and what you once were is not who you are today. The past may offer lessons, but it is not the truth, just as the future is nothing more than imagination. Neither the past nor the future exists in this moment. The only reality we have is the present.

Let me illustrate this with a story.

A boy from a small, middle-class family, burdened by family responsibilities and carrying a few dreams in his empty pockets, ventures to big cities like Delhi, Bangalore, or Mumbai in search of opportunity. His resume might not boast degrees from Harvard or Oxford, nor experience at elite companies like Google or IBM. But what he lacks in credentials, he makes up for with ambition and resolve. His dreams are vast, and his spirit unwavering. He envisions creating an ecosystem in the business world that not only brings prosperity to others but also shapes the future with his ideals and policies. With this vision in mind, he makes a firm decision—not to settle, not to be satisfied, until he becomes a success on his own terms.

'It's a profound truth that to soar on the wings of your dreams, you need a foundation built on real, ground-level experience. Financial and mental challenges are an entirely different story.'

By this stage in his journey, he had realised one crucial thing—before anything else, he needed to invest in himself. He began his career as an intern at an IT solutions company. From there, he moved into an executive role, gaining valuable experience in marketing and sales across one or two companies. His dedication and commitment took him through various business domains, and within nine to ten years, he had worked his way into senior management. Life seemed perfect—he was earning a seven-figure salary, had a respectable position, and could comfortably manage both his professional and personal responsibilities. Whenever someone met him, they would say, 'You've made it! Your life is set.'

His friends and family began to see him as the epitome of success. And yet, there was still something missing, something incomplete. Even today, he often finds himself reflecting back to that determined 21-year-old boy who had left home vowing not to rest until he had truly succeeded. Were position, prestige, and wealth the only yardsticks for measuring success? Did these external markers of achievement mean he had reached his goal? Time and again, he found himself asking, 'What's next? Is this all there is?'

The most profound and intriguing truth of life is that what we often see as the end is, in fact, just the beginning. Think of a seed—you plant it, you nurture it, you don't sit idly, hoping for rain by chance. Slowly, that seed sprouts into a small plant. With proper care, it grows, eventually blossoming and bearing fruit. But simply tasting the fruit of success cannot be the final destination. The transformation of that fruit back into a seed is part of nature's cycle, a never-ending ecosystem.

Consider this: the seed of your idea—your thought— faces countless trials, enduring various seasons and storms as it grows from a sprout to a sapling, from a sapling to a plant, and finally to a fruit-bearing tree. Only after weathering these challenges does it evolve into something tangible—a vision, an organisation, a company. The fruits of your labour embody your thoughts, carrying the essence of your ideas. But success isn't just about survival in the competitive business ecosystem; it's about creating new seeds from those fruits. Seeds that carry forward the legacy of your vision, your company—pushing it toward the future, ensuring that what you've built doesn't just survive but thrives long after you've moved on.

The boy who had seemingly established himself at one point began to question his fleeting success. In truth, his ideas were only just beginning to take root in the vast ecosystem of business. He had mastered the technical aspects, learned the tricks of the trade, but his thoughts had yet to fully materialise. He still had to cultivate them, to weather the storms of change and adversity. What he once believed to be the end of his journey was merely the starting point. This is the process of evolution—of change. Whenever you find yourself asking, 'What's next?' understand that you are on the verge of transformation.

The first truth we need to accept is that *business is simply a system*, and the process of change is the fundamental condition for survival in that system. When we launch a company or start a business, we must design a sustainable ecosystem in which our company can thrive for years to come. To do that, change is inevitable.

Consider companies like Amazon, now one of the most valuable in the world—it started as nothing more than an online bookstore. YouTube began as a dating platform, and Netflix originally dealt with DVD rentals. These businesses evolved by recognising and adapting to the demands of their time, and today they are industry giants.

But here's something to keep in mind: this process isn't simple. If you declare, 'I want to implement change,' it won't happen overnight. The first step is to move forward, assess upcoming challenges, create strategies, and anticipate future risks. Sometimes, though, change arrives without giving you the luxury of preparation.

Did you know? Companies that frequently pivot or reinvent themselves are 30% more likely to outperform their competitors in the long run. Change isn't just an option—it's essential for survival.

The same thing happened to Anubhav. The company he worked for became entangled in a conflict between investors and shareholders, ultimately leading to its closure. At this crossroads, Anubhav faced two choices. One was to search for another job, retreating back into his comfort zone. The other was to carve a new path, one where he could create opportunities not just for himself, but for others as well. He chose the latter. Anubhav returned to his hometown and launched a startup. His venture, focused on food products, supplied snacks to various offices across the city. Around this time, he also got married, marking a new chapter in his life. This was a period of intense change — both personally and professionally.

Amidst the struggles of his fledgling company — starved for financial resources — Anubhav faced the pressure of new responsibilities, uncertainty about the future, and the drive to establish himself. But perhaps the most painful challenge was the shifting attitudes of those around him. Returning home after a long time, he soon realised that people's perception of him began to change. Those closest to him started viewing him as a failure, ready to write off his efforts. While it's easy to claim that we don't care what others think, their words have the power to undermine even the strongest resolve. They can shake your confidence to the core.

This is one of the harsh realities of small towns — dreams and new ideas may be born here, but the sky is often too limited for those dreams to truly soar. Anubhav's ambitions, to explore the corporate food supply chain and create a successful business, collided with the traditional expectations of his surroundings. A middle-class teacher father often wants his son to become a doctor or an engineer, to study for exams, or join the civil services. A shopkeeper, on the other hand, would expect his son to carry on the family business. Even if one breaks free from these societal expectations, the lack of resources in such places makes nurturing a business even more challenging.

Anubhav's hometown wasn't the right environment for his entrepreneurial vision. The idea of catering to the food demands of corporate offices through an efficient supply chain didn't gain traction in this setting. Limited resources and a collapsing supply system led to the failure of his business. It was his first experience of failure. What is the first taste of failure like? Many would say it's bitter, but I say it's enlightening. Failure reveals the truth. It acts like a mirror, reflecting not just where we went wrong but who we truly are.

People often say, 'I worked so hard, but luck wasn't on my side.' Those who attribute failure to luck are often unwilling to learn from it. Failure, in fact, shines a light on our shortcomings. It exposes the mistakes that hold us back from success. We cannot achieve anything by relying solely on luck. The road to success is paved with relentless effort.

It's possible that Anubhav wasn't successful in his first attempt, but that doesn't mean he should stop trying. The past cannot be changed, no matter how much this society judges us by our wins and losses. However, the past can be our greatest teacher. Success and failure are both outcomes of past efforts. While success shows us new possibilities, failure forces us to confront our mistakes and prevent repeating them.

Understand this: success and failure are two sides of the same coin. You may not win on the first or even second toss, but eventually, the coin will flip in your favour. That's why I say, success isn't something handed to us—it's something we weave carefully, day by day, through persistence and learning from our setbacks.

But Anubhav wasn't in a position to fail, nor did he have the financial cushion to try something else. After the collapse of his company, his situation only worsened. He was both financially and emotionally devastated. Despite his efforts to climb out of this dark phase, each attempt felt like the desperate floundering of a fish stranded on the sand, far from the ocean. Life had thrown him into a crisis, and no clear way forward seemed visible.

Anubhav's mind was a whirlwind of thoughts. Sometimes he imagined retreating to a quiet hill station and opening a small shop, while at other times he considered earning a living by driving a taxi. Yet, through all the chaos, the fire within him—the drive to achieve something meaningful—never dimmed.

There's a beautiful truth that resonates with such times: 'If a person wants to avoid falling into despair, they must keep moving, keep working.' Despite the adversities, Anubhav's vision of doing something significant fuelled his resolve. He needed to find a way to survive the present, to regain his footing. So, he once again set out for Bangalore. His goal remained the same—to make something big of his life, regardless of the obstacles ahead.

We must understand a fundamental truth right from the start: whatever we aim to achieve in life, whatever we are currently pursuing, we must first know the motive behind it. The purpose with which you create a company, the direction it needs to head, where you envision it reaching, and how long it will thrive—all of these are shaped by your motive. Without clarity on this, setting a goal is impossible.

Imagine setting sail on a boat without knowing the purpose of the voyage—how long you'll travel, in which direction you'll go, or what your final destination is. Without answers to these questions, you're bound to drift aimlessly. Even if you bring aboard the most skilled sailor, without a clear purpose, the boat will simply return to the same shore where you began.

This is why, from day one of starting a company, you must also grasp this essential truth: what is your motive? Later in this book, we will explore the concept of motive in greater detail, but the clarity of your purpose is what sets the foundation for everything that follows.

Even after the early setback in his career, Anubhav didn't lose heart. His vision remained clear—he was determined to do something big. Once again, he made his way back to Bangalore. There, he secured a position at a leading marketing firm, which gave him the stability and courage to face his current challenges. Alongside his job, he laid the foundation of his own marketing company.

During times of recovery, it's essential to remain vigilant. It's in these moments that we must grasp an important truth: life is cyclical. Just as day follows night, bad times will eventually give way to good ones. This understanding underscores the need to always stay aware of our surroundings, our actions, and our purpose. Only when you stay conscious can you recognise opportunities that might otherwise slip by unnoticed. It is this awareness that keeps your goal in focus, guiding you toward the right path. Without clarity, you may stray from your course. But with awareness, you learn from past mistakes, turn present challenges into opportunities, and anticipate the future.

Another fundamental truth is that no one can run their company forever. At some point, you will have to step away. What truly matters is how long you intend to keep your company thriving. Human life is finite, and the question arises—what happens after you leave? What will become of the company you built with vision and dedication? Many believe that their children will carry on their legacy, but there's no guarantee they'll share the same passion or interest. This is why it's crucial to continually confront these truths, preparing not just for the present but for the future of what you've created.

The purpose of this book is to open your eyes to the truths that are often overlooked. I aim to guide you on how to build a company with a solid foundation—one that can endure into the future. Every founder dreams of creating a business that outlives them, and I'm sure you share this vision as well. We all strive for something lasting. We seek love until the end, we chase wealth until our final breath, and we yearn to reach the farthest corners of the universe, constantly searching for the ultimate destination. In the end, we all desire something better. If I were to ask how long you would want your creation, your company, to thrive, your answer would likely be, 'Until the end'. But you cannot reach that point unless you align with the truth.

Truth is an internal compass, something we all aspire to attain in the form of success. But where do we falter?

Why do companies crumble after achieving success? Is a startup's lifespan limited to four or five years? There are companies that have lasted a millennium—what is the secret to surviving in this ever-changing ecosystem? In this book, we'll explore these questions. We will also follow the journey of someone who brought a company into existence after tremendous struggle, yet the uncertainty of its future still looms. Will they succeed in their ultimate purpose? The answer remains unknown for now.

Remember, everything created in this world is bound to come to an end. It may be disheartening to think that the company you've built with so much passion, dedication, and vision will eventually meet its demise, but this is a truth we must face. The real question is: what is its expiry date? From my own continuous experience, I can reveal this truth. If you allow me the time, I can tell you with confidence why *'Your company is going to shut down.'* And as we journey through this book, I hope you will grasp this truth with clarity and understanding.

2

Karma: Drive Success Forward

———•———

'TO BE HONEST, THE JOURNEY OF BUSINESS IS SHROUDED in a fog of uncertainty. If you truly want to enjoy this path, you must ensure that your actions serve as the guiding light.'

As business leaders, we are driven by certain goals that we are determined to achieve at all costs. We feel a constant urgency to reach these milestones, eager to conquer one summit after another. We don't have a hundred lifetimes to fulfil these ambitions; we strive to explore every dimension of the market within the span of this one life. Each day presents the desire to innovate, to uncover the market's hidden opportunities from fresh perspectives. In pursuit of this, we tirelessly explore every avenue, leaving no stone unturned in our quest for success. We seek to establish ourselves through relentless efforts, seizing every opportunity that comes our way.

However, we must accept the reality that our time on this earth is limited. No matter how hard we push, we cannot do it all. Even if we build vast networks and connect countless people to our cause, our work will inevitably encounter boundaries. Yet, despite these limitations, we can leave behind a legacy through actions that resonate beyond our own time—actions whose impact can be felt and cherished by humanity for generations to come.

I am not at all surprised that some companies have endured for over a thousand years. Their longevity is neither a stroke of luck nor a miracle. It may seem miraculous to outsiders because no one can replicate their success by simply following a prescribed formula. If you look at the market today, there are countless brands offering the same product, yet only a select few rise to the top. The formula may appear straightforward: slice the potatoes, fry them, package them, and sell them. Sure, the marketing tactics might differ, but the basic process is the same. However, even if we all follow that same formula, success is far from guaranteed. The secret to these companies' enduring success lies not in some mystical force, but in the power of their actions—the karma they've accumulated, whose impact has resonated through generations.

It's a fact that in a world of billions, only about four per cent are considered the wealthiest, yet they control over 50 per cent of the global market, directly or indirectly. It's human nature to aspire to be part of that elite group. We eagerly try to emulate their success formulas, believing that by following in their footsteps, success will be ours as well. But in reality, the path to success is often obscured by a thick fog of uncertainty. The reason that fog exists is our desire for rapid results. We're impatient, wanting to be counted among those four per cent—and not just to reach them, but to surpass them.

The truth is, if I were to focus on every ambition I've ever had, it would likely take a hundred lifetimes to fulfil them all. That's why we feel the need to outrun time itself. In this rush, we often risk more than we realise. But never forget—those who are successful today earned it through years, if not decades, of sustained action. If you wish to taste the same success, you must carve your own path. It's your actions that will dispel the fog, your efforts that will illuminate the road ahead. No one else will do the work for you, and success will only come if you commit fully to the journey.

This raises a critical question: how do we act in a way that guarantees not only success but also fulfilment? How do we ensure that the seeds we plant today will bear fruit tomorrow?

'To me, success is the outcome of my entire body of work—I am reaping the harvest of what I once sowed.'

We need to grasp the fundamental reason behind why we engage in karma (action). If you think you're solely responsible for driving your actions, you're mistaken. It's not you, but your thoughts that guide you. Karma stems from the thoughts we nurture, not from any external source. The process is simple: you conceive an idea, and then you take steps to turn that idea into reality. Nothing we do is random. Our subconscious mind is constantly collecting thoughts born from our experiences and imagination, and the actions we take are the reflection of those thoughts. Whether these actions will yield results depends on how well we cultivate and nurture our thoughts, and how consistently we act upon them.

Every decision, right or wrong, originates in the mind. That's why I believe that if we nourish our thoughts with integrity and awareness, our actions will inevitably bear fruit. Karma is the tool by which a person shapes their life, moulds their character, and presents their identity to the world.

Now, let's address the next question: why does a person engage in karma? When people ask, 'What do you do?' they're not just inquiring about your occupation; they are measuring you. They're assessing your wealth, status, and influence through the lens of your actions. In essence, they're evaluating your character. Like it or not, much of what we do is driven by this constant need to measure up to societal standards.

If we delve into the deepest ambition of human beings, it's the desire for validation. We want to be praised, admired, and seen as superior in some way. We crave recognition, and our actions often become geared toward earning that approval. We want to leave a mark, to be remembered. And so, much of what we do is simply a reaction to this fundamental desire for acknowledgment, for influence. Our actions, then, become a reflection of our pursuit of this validation.

Karma, in its truest sense, is the work that propels you toward your goal—an objective that is worthy of your dedication. It's a purpose so significant that your actions are aligned with it at every step. If possible, write down these objectives, these thoughts that fuel your ambition, and place them where you see them daily—whether on the walls of your office or your home. Let these thoughts take root and grow within you, day and night. Remember, all great achievements begin as simple ideas in the mind, nurtured through continuous effort. In essence, karma is the stove on which we cook the results of our labour; what you serve is what you've prepared through your actions.

If you desire to fulfil your purpose and build an influential persona, I suggest adopting this principle in your life: 'From idea to action, from action to habit, from habit to character, and from character to influence.' I can assure you that if your actions are aligned with this journey, the results will follow. You will undoubtedly find yourself among the ranks of influential people. However, it's important to understand that transforming an idea into a fully formed character takes time. Just as a seed doesn't turn into a fruit-bearing tree overnight, ideas also require nurturing and patience.

The maturation of an idea takes time, just as a fruit requires time to ripen from a seedling. During this period, the fruit undergoes countless transformations, adapting and evolving with each stage. Business works in much the same way, and that's why I emphasise repeatedly that 'Adaptation to change is the first step toward success. Those who mould their ideas and actions to fit the ever-changing landscape will eventually reap the rewards. But whether those rewards are sweet or bitter, whether your efforts lead to success or failure, will ultimately be determined by your character.'

Character is built by nurturing your thoughts. Regardless of the circumstances—whether joyful or challenging—what truly matters is how we tend to our inner world. A company, like any living thing, goes through various stages. Consider a small plant; it requires constant care and attention until it grows sturdy and tall. During this period, don't we prune it, removing the weak, withered branches? These fragile branches are like our fleeting desires, the distractions that come with every thought. Desires are inevitable, but the key to growth lies in knowing which ones to let go of. And for how long? Until that small plant matures into a tree that bears sweet fruit, we must not waver from our purpose for even a moment. The concept of survival of the fittest echoes this idea—only the strong, the virtuous, and the determined will thrive. You must nurture the thoughts and desires that align with your purpose and have the courage to let go of those that don't.

Karma is the action you take to bring your thoughts to life. That's why I say, if your intentions are sincere and your thoughts are grounded in truth, your actions will inevitably yield results—they will be fruitful. Imagine you have a genuine desire to contribute to the field of education, to uplift society through learning. What will you do? You'll begin by acquiring knowledge, earning degrees, perhaps offering tuitions to a few children, or becoming a teacher at a school. Each of these steps is karma. And if, through your efforts, even one child is able to receive an education, then that is the harvest of your thought—a tangible outcome born from your actions.

Now it's up to you to decide how far you want your thoughts to reach and how widely you wish to spread them. Always remember, there is no limit to your thoughts. They evolve and transform each day; they are inherently dynamic. Therefore, it's crucial that you avoid becoming bound by your actions—do not let yourself get trapped in the confines of karma. There's a significant difference between being karma-bound and achieving karma completion. If your karma remains incomplete, I can confidently say, 'Your company is destined to falter.'

So, how do we ensure that karma is complete? The straightforward answer is to avoid becoming bound by it. We must keep our ideas fluid and allow them to flourish. Any actions that inhibit the growth of your ideas are binding; they are a form of karma that restricts your potential.

The true blossoming of ideas is what karma represents. Thus, only those who can transform a new idea into reality can be deemed successful entrepreneurs. Conversely, actions that stifle this blossoming are chains that bind.

Let's revisit the earlier example. You embark on your journey with the noble intention of making a difference in education—of uplifting society through learning. Eventually, you secure a position as a teacher, enjoying all the comforts and a handsome salary that come with it. At that moment, you might feel your life is complete.

But in doing so, you have inadvertently confined your thoughts. While you may be educating a hundred students and feeling fulfilled, I ask you: when your original resolution was to enlighten society, why limit your impact to just a handful of individuals or a single role?

You could have expanded your impact by becoming a university professor or even starting your own school through perseverance and hard work. By limiting your ideas, you created a bond—a constraint that holds your potential captive. This bond is akin to a contract that ties your aspirations to a specific path. But life isn't about untangling these bonds; the more you try to disentangle, the more ensnared you become. The essence of life is struggle—the same struggle a tree endures as it transforms from seed to sprout, from sprout to stem, branches, and finally to fruit. This journey of growth cannot be bypassed; struggles must be embraced.

When Lord Krishna advises us *karam karo, phal ki chinta mat karo,* he encourages us to live fully in the present. Embrace the now, engage deeply in your work, and lose yourself in the joy of the moment, free from worries about tomorrow. Your relationships and responsibilities should be approached with practicality; true devotion belongs to your thoughts and purpose—the driving forces of your life.

This world is a tapestry of aspirations and questions. Just when you believe you've solved one issue, another will present itself. As you attain a certain position, new goals will inevitably emerge. You cannot escape this cycle, for it defines our existence. The struggle is inherent; it arises from an inner self that seeks answers beyond any constraints. There's a part of you that yearns for clarity amidst the chaos, and it is this part that propels you forward on your journey.

Marriage is often referred to as a bond, a contract between two souls. Before marriage, people match horoscopes, assess compatibility, and examine qualities. Why? The reasoning behind this is that when qualities align, thoughts are more likely to harmonise. And when thoughts are in sync, it becomes easier to navigate life's questions together. When marriages end, we frequently hear that 'their thoughts didn't align.' This is why it's important to surround yourself with those whose thoughts resonate with your own, whether in personal or professional partnerships. What is a job, after all, but a contract? You exchange your labour for a salary, working in alignment with your company's ideas. This is how the world functions—businesses, systems, all operate this way. The bonds of karma are our duties, and trying to escape them only traps us in our own minds, tangled in our thoughts. That's why I urge you to engage in them fully. Give meaning to life's struggles. These karmic bonds, these challenges, need space to unfold because they allow your thoughts to evolve and your character to take shape, creating something truly influential. Only when your actions are free from all bonds can they be called complete.

Take Anubhav, for example—he's willing to take risks. He has faced many phases in life, most of which have brought him disappointment and failure. But his thoughts and ambitions are big. He finds himself in Bangalore once again, searching for an opportunity. Everyone faces such moments in life when they stray from their goals, their purpose. People often call this diversion a necessity or helplessness. This helplessness can take many forms—be it responsibility, a job, societal pressure, or even personal desires. These are the karmic bonds, but I call them the truth of time.

I've already shared with you that the present cannot be ignored. The current circumstances may not be in your favour, and the time might demand something different, but that doesn't mean you should lock away your thoughts and bury your purpose deep within yourself. Doing so is dangerous. I call it dangerous because it creates an internal conflict, a war within. Many people fall into this trap. They become so consumed by external battles that they lose sight of the conflicts brewing inside. They fight the small, external battles while neglecting the more significant inner ones, unable to discern which struggle truly matters. The real battle is freeing yourself from the negative thoughts and disturbances that hinder the completion of your actions. As you begin to address the conflict within, you become more capable of handling the challenges outside.

Anubhav was facing challenges much like many do in life. With the determination to achieve something meaningful, despite the weight of previous failures, he once again found himself in Bangalore, seeking a new path after an earlier setback. Failure in life isn't unusual—it's part of the journey. Every individual strives to reach their goals in their own way; some succeed, some fail. That's why it's said that success and failure aren't determined by ability but by effort. Success, much like the flip of a coin, hinges on how persistent your efforts are. The real test isn't whether you fail, but how well you can carry the burden of that failure.

What is the weight of failure, really? Does it feel so heavy that it crushes all hope? Does it leave a mark so dark that it clouds your judgement? Or does it feel like chains—chains that you struggle to break free from, a battle that slowly wears you down? Failure brings a darkness that can feel overwhelming, where even your own shadow seems absent. In that darkness, you may search for those who once stood by you—relatives who praised you, friends whose doors were always open—but now, all you find is silence. The doors are shut, the voices quiet, and hope feels distant, as though it has abandoned you entirely.

In that darkness, you might wander, clutching to faith, only to be shown time and time again that the world places little value on it. What value is there in such darkness?

And yet, all it takes is a single spark—a small flame of light—to break through. But that light is not found outside in the world; it's found within, waiting to be uncovered. Many spend their lives searching for that light elsewhere, waiting for a saviour or a solution, but all they find is fog—disappointment, frustration, distrust. These external forces only aim to drag you further down. That is why I say, keep the flame of your thoughts burning within. To keep that flame alive is your karma, and it takes relentless passion and stubbornness to ensure it never dies.

When you pursue your purpose with unwavering determination, when you let that passion drive you, your thoughts begin to glow. They spread outward, becoming habits, actions, and eventually, reality. These habits are what give your ideas the space to take root, to flourish. This is why I say, keep moving forward. Karma has the power to lift every burden, to dissolve every obstacle like mist in the air.

Anubhav decided to not stop until he achieved his purpose. Satisfaction, he realised, is another challenge altogether. True satisfaction can only come from within; nothing in the world can provide it unless you feel it inside. The mind is like a child—innocent, but stubborn. When a child is fixated on the moon, no number of toys or treats can distract them. Parents may offer everything they can, but it's futile. Similarly, this is a formula for success: until you reach your goal, hold on to that stubbornness. It's acceptable to fall a hundred times on the path to your destination. You may lose your way countless times, but giving up is not an option. If you can't find the road, forge a new one. If you get lost, start again. Just don't stop. Stopping is where karma binds you, trapping you in place.

If you ever wonder whether your efforts have come to fruition, look inward. Ask yourself, what was the original purpose behind starting something as significant as your company? Have you achieved what you set out to do? The hunger, the drive that made you set aside personal desires and embark on this journey—has it been fulfilled? Reflect on whether your thoughts have found satisfaction at the end of this path.

If the answer is yes, then ask yourself another question: 'What will happen to this company that I nurtured like a daughter, raised with values, and invested my whole life into?' You've sacrificed so much for its future, saved every penny, but is that enough? You won't have a clear answer, because no one can see the future. Only your thoughts can travel there. If your actions are shackled by karmic bonds, preventing your ideas from moving into the future, then I can say with certainty, '*Your company is going to shut down.*'

3

Untie the Knots of Karma

———•———

'IN THIS BUSINESS JOURNEY OF FULFILLING OUR PURPOSE, NO matter how wise or determined we may be, we cannot reach the summit of success if our actions are bound by limitations. True freedom in our actions is essential to ascend to the highest levels of achievement.'

As a business leader, I deeply aspire for my company to reach a state of perfection. I envision a company that excels in every facet of the market—internally fortified with a strong, resilient structure, and externally tuned to understand the evolving needs of our clients, delivering solutions that make a real impact. Like every founder, I dream of building the ideal company, one that checks every box of success. But that vision represents the ultimate destination. Right now, we are still on the path, navigating toward that summit. We are not yet whole—there are still many pieces to assemble, many lessons to learn. Our journey is one of progress, and with each right decision, each step forward, the path to success becomes clearer.

The key to success lies in the harmonious alignment of our purpose, wisdom, and actions. These three must converge naturally for our steps to confidently lead us forward. Without this unity, we remain incomplete. For example, someone might have immense passion for their purpose but lack the wisdom to realise it. Another person may be highly skilled and prudent in their work but lack a clear purpose. Similarly, one may possess deep knowledge but have no drive to put it into action. In these scenarios, something vital is missing, and we remain fragmented.

To dive into the vast ocean of success, we must come together—our purpose, wisdom, and actions working in unison. We must strive for wholeness in this journey. However, we must begin with the acceptance that we are incomplete, understanding that it is through our imperfections and efforts to align that true growth and success will emerge.

To begin from incompleteness means to start exactly where you are, and to progress from there. If you're on foot, there's no shame in that—walk at your own pace. When the time comes, push forward toward a bicycle. If you're riding a bicycle, that speed is sufficient for now—travel at that pace until you're ready for a car. Once you're in a car, accelerate towards a ship. The key is to keep moving forward, constantly progressing. Success isn't about how fast you're moving; it's about forward momentum. Progress means always striving to be better than you were yesterday. Wherever you find yourself today, aim to be ahead of that point tomorrow. Success is not a destination but an ongoing journey of becoming a better version of yourself. As long as you keep this vehicle of life moving at your own pace, rest assured, *'the destination is never far.'*

The real question, then, is how do we choose the right path to reach the pinnacle of success, to arrive at our destination? As I mentioned in the first chapter, each person must find their own unique path to success. Let me expand on that idea. The fundamental essence of life is the pursuit of happiness. Happiness, in fact, can be considered our ultimate goal. Everything we think, plan, or do is ultimately driven by our desire to stay in a state of happiness. We engage in certain activities because they bring us joy and fulfilment. Therefore, when choosing a path, it's vital to pursue something that naturally draws you in, something that aligns with your interests and passions. Choose a path that you are deeply connected to, one that feels meaningful and fulfilling. When you align your journey with your true inclinations, success is no longer an external goal but a natural outcome of living in harmony with your inner purpose.

The second point is that walking on your chosen path with awareness and intention is your karma. This karma is your vehicle. Without karma—without a vehicle—how can you expect to reach your destination? Imagine you need to travel a hundred miles, but you're unsure about how to get there. The journey would be full of uncertainty. To travel, it's essential to understand the means, the vehicle. But there's more to it: you must also master those means. Mastery is impossible without practice. Any journey is only truly successful when both the vehicle and the driver are in perfect sync. Perfection comes with practice—repeated, consistent effort. If you set a goal in life, you cannot achieve it unless you continuously practise and refine your actions. Let's consider our business: can we achieve results if we don't practise, adapt, and strive every day? Consistency and persistence, trying different methods, and seeking better outcomes all contribute to mastery. Karma is perfected through continuous practice.

Success is synonymous with perfection, integrity, and reaching your ultimate destination. You cannot achieve success while remaining incomplete. To succeed, your thoughts, objectives, discretion, and intellect must be whole and aligned. This completeness can only be attained through relentless practice and a commitment to refinement.

Instead of focusing only on what perfect karma looks like, we should also consider how our actions contribute to our journey towards success. We know that humans cannot live without doing karma, but we must also recognise that it is not merely us driving our actions. Something deeper within us guides us—our thoughts. For example, if you feel thirsty, a thought arises telling you to drink water. Only then do you extend your hand, pick up the glass, and quench your thirst. No action occurs without reason; everything we do is tied to our thoughts. These thoughts arise continuously, and throughout life, we perform various actions to satisfy them.

In the business world, there are countless paths to success, and each person who has reached the top will advocate for the path they followed. Look at the world's wealthiest individuals—those who achieved success in technology will say that technology is the best path. Those in manufacturing will argue for that industry, while those in automobiles will claim it is the finest route. None of them are wrong, because people can only recommend the paths they know, the ones that worked for them. They can't speak for paths they've never walked. That's why you'll hear so much advice: 'Follow this path, avoid that one. This business is more profitable, that one is risky.' You'll be bombarded with opinions, distractions, and directions, and it's crucial to stay vigilant and make choices with clarity. Ultimately, the path you choose must resonate with your thoughts and intentions, because that is the only way to ensure your karma aligns with your success.

When you embark on a business journey, it's crucial to be clear about which paths to follow and which ones to avoid, ensuring that you don't get distracted. Often, knowing what *not* to do is more important than knowing what to do. Any action that derails you from your goal, or that hinders the success of your company, becomes an obstacle—a form of karmic bondage.

In my own journey, I've often been advised against pursuing business. Some say it's a difficult road, while others claim certain industries aren't worth the effort. I've encountered countless voices suggesting that I try my hand at something else, claiming I'd achieve more elsewhere. As many opinions as there are people. But we must not lose focus—we must avoid getting sidetracked.

Anubhav, too, faced these distractions at one point in his life. When he decided to start his own company in his hometown, he went through similar challenges. His father, a secondary school teacher, had always hoped he would pursue a secure government job, perhaps in administrative services. Though his father never outright discouraged him from doing business, he still believed it to be a riskier, less secure path. To him, a life in business seemed unstable. While Anubhav made some attempts at joining administrative services, his heart was always set on something much larger. From the very beginning, he envisioned building a system that could generate employment for young people in smaller towns and villages—those with talent and dedication but who lacked opportunities due to limited resources.

When you come from such places and try to make your way in big cities, the path is steep and full of sacrifices. Anubhav had to stake a great deal in the early stages of chasing his dream. He gave up the pursuit of government exams, moved to a big city for work, and then eventually returned to lay the foundation for his first company in his hometown. With just a few friends and limited resources, they built a system that eventually failed. But this failure came after significant personal sacrifice—he had already put so much at stake.

Despite the setbacks and voices that urged him to take a different path, Anubhav stayed true to his vision, knowing that veering off course would only lead to karmic entanglements. His perseverance laid the foundation for future success. The lesson here is clear: success requires focus, resilience, and the courage to stay on the right path, no matter the distractions or challenges.

One of the primary reasons Anubhav's company had to close was because the friends he partnered with had different goals and visions. Each of them was pulled toward their own area of expertise, their interests confined to the fields they knew best. It was like a boat with multiple rowers, each paddling in different directions—the boat inevitably sinks. To create a successful company, it's essential that the vision, goals, wisdom, and actions of everyone involved align and move together in the same direction. As long as the company is fragmented and scattered, the journey will feel disjointed and distracted, making it nearly impossible to arrive at any meaningful destination.

In my own business journey, I've often heard people say, 'Don't go into business; it's a difficult path,' or 'Business people lack integrity.' It baffles me how many misconceptions surround entrepreneurship, and I wonder how many more falsehoods will continue to spread. Sometimes, I try to gauge people's perceptions of business, and when I listen to their views, it feels like they think entrepreneurship is a web of deceit, where one is constantly entangled in negative forces. I'm left wondering, what does anyone gain by spreading such misconceptions? Why do people have a natural tendency to misunderstand things? Why do we willingly remain part of the crowd, mindlessly following the spectacle before us? It's like there's a show being played out, a crowd gathering, the performer leading the dance, and we're dancing along—without even asking why. This is an army of people caught in madness, constantly seeking thrills and adventure, but has anyone ever stopped to ask why we chase these things? Are our lives truly that mysterious? Thoughts come to us, but do we ever stop to question where they come from or why they emerge?

I often hear my father's friends talk about their children's futures, picturing them as doctors, engineers, or in administrative services. Rarely do I hear anyone say they want their child to become a businessperson. When I ask why, some even get angry. It's beyond their understanding that life itself is business. What does a person do with their actions throughout their life? They engage in the exchange of ideas. And what is that exchange if not business?

You might have built a large company, honing your skills and talents to grow both yourself and the business. But why all the hard work, why the struggle? What's the purpose behind it? If anyone says, 'I'm doing this to secure my existence,' I challenge them to ask themselves if they've truly understood what their existence even means. What will become of this life they've built around preserving that existence after they're gone? Have you asked what will happen to your company's existence once you're no longer here? What will happen to the vision and objectives you've cultivated? Remember this: your actions determine how far your thoughts will travel. Your actions are the vehicle by which your ideas are carried forward. In the end, it is through your deeds that the legacy of your thoughts and goals will continue to thrive.

Everyone dreams of immortality—every founder wishes for their company to endure through time. But have you ever asked yourself, what is the path to immortality? What are the true means to achieve it? There are companies that have stood strong for centuries. Why have they survived for so long? Look deeper. Don't settle for surface-level answers like 'the product is good.' Sure, that's what most people will say, but why is the product good? Challenge yourself to dig deeper into this question. Imagine filling a bottle with poison and offering it in the marketplace—you will still find buyers. This is why the market is often referred to as the 'market of possibilities.' There is nothing that won't find a buyer in this world. So, ask yourself this: if this particular product didn't exist, would life continue? The answer is usually yes. Then where does the distinction between 'good' and 'bad' come from? This is why I say: no creation is inherently good or bad. Every product is complete in itself. What may be incomplete are your thoughts and actions. The product you create is a reflection of the clarity and commitment you put into it. If you bring something into the market and it doesn't sell, it's easy to blame the market. But have you ever paused to reflect on the process that led to that creation? The result is always a direct outcome of the effort, intention, and skill you applied.

The first key to success is to remain unwavering in your objective. To achieve greatness, you must nurture thoughts that align with your goal. Life will throw countless distractions and conflicting ideas your way, but you must stay firm in your purpose. In the business world, temptations are everywhere, but you cannot afford to stray from your path. This integrity, this unwavering focus on your goal, strengthens your resolve and sets you on a path to success.

The second key is that dedication surpasses even determination. Thoughts will come and go, bubbling up like fleeting ideas. But how committed you are to translating that single thought into action defines your success. It's not just about having a resolution—it's about dedicating yourself fully to it. Your level of dedication directly influences the outcome of your efforts.

Dedication is rooted in faith. You must believe in the path you are walking, in the work you are doing, and in your own abilities. Without genuine faith in your mission, you will never truly dedicate yourself to it. Faith fuels dedication, and dedication ensures success. When you believe wholeheartedly in your journey, only then can you give yourself fully to it and achieve the heights you seek.

Dedication means love. True dedication to your work awakens a deep sense of love for it. I often hear entrepreneurs and friends proudly say, 'I love my company, my job, my position.' And that's great—there *should* be love in what we do. But have you ever paused to ask yourself, why do you feel this love? Is it genuine, or is attachment disguised as love? Because if there is attachment, then it's not love in the truest sense. What is love, really? It's pure dedication. It's where Krishna becomes Radha, and Radha becomes Krishna—that is love. To be entirely dedicated to someone or something is love. Yet, in today's world, the meaning of love has become distorted. Love has become synonymous with pleasure, with enjoyment. But where there is enjoyment for the sake of pleasure, true dedication vanishes. If the work you do is primarily tied to the joy it brings you, then that love is shallow. Nowadays, people equate love with personal gratification. 'I love this person because she's beautiful,' they'll say, but underneath that declaration, desires are swirling in their minds. It seems like if they don't satisfy these desires, everything will lose meaning. When love becomes about fulfilling desires, it turns into mere enjoyment—love, in its purest form, gets lost.

True love, like Krishna's, is when he sees Radha in every being. This is the ultimate form of surrender. When you surrender in such a way, you will see only your beloved in everything and everyone. There will be no attachment to their form, their nature, or their outward appearance. At that point, both become one. When you're fully dedicated to your work, you and that work merge into one. Then, the work is not something external—it becomes a part of you. That's love. This is what Krishna and Radha's unity represents.

Dedication is the truth—the understanding of reality as it is. When something else takes its place, that's attachment, not love. And attachment is karmic bondage. When you bind yourself to anything that distracts you from your true purpose, that is the bondage of karma.

Ask yourself: You weren't created without reason. Discover your role in this world. Seek out the purpose for which you were made. And here's the thing—you don't need to search for this truth outside of yourself, because the answer is already within. I've seen many talented people embark on endless searches for success. They often get lost along the way. The throngs we see crowding around business counsellors, gurus, and spiritual leaders, seeking a path to success—these are people disconnected from the truth that all the answers they seek are within them. The road to success begins exactly where you stand. Yet, what surprises me most is how often these seekers are offered new distractions, new forms of bondage that lead to nothing but disillusionment. Even more startling is how readily we accept these paths, only to find more disappointment.

I recall a story I read once, and I'd like to share it with you...

A monkey was born—just an ordinary monkey, with two hands, two legs, and a healthy body, perfectly normal in every way. But soon after its birth, tragedy struck—the monkey's mother passed away. One day, a juggler spotted the baby monkey, took him home, and fastened a chain around his neck. From that moment on, the chain never left him. The monkey grew up with this chain, and as time passed, he accepted it as part of his very being. In fact, he became so accustomed to it that he believed this chain was like a third arm. The bond was so ingrained in his mind that he could not separate the chain from his sense of self. Wherever the monkey went, he walked as though he had three arms—the two he was born with and the third, imagined one, around his neck. He clung to this chain so tightly that he couldn't even conceive of a life without it.

Opportunities for freedom came to the monkey many times, but he never took them. Why? Because he had convinced himself that this chain was an essential part of him, part of who he was. As the years went by, the monkey grew older, and he became an influential figure among other monkeys. He was respected, looked up to, and many came to him for advice. Parents even sent their children to this three-armed monkey to learn from him. But what kind of advice could this monkey, so attached to his chain, offer? Naturally, he believed the other monkeys were lacking something. He would look at them with concern and ask, 'Where's your third arm? You're missing something. You must fill that gap in your life.'

As his fame spread, this monkey started to convince others that his chain—his imagined third arm—was something extraordinary, something others needed too. He made them believe that without it, they were incomplete. He created an entire system, a belief that to be whole, one must possess this 'third arm.' Soon, schools and colleges were set up, promising that through education, young monkeys could 'fill the gap' in their lives. Markets and shops emerged, all devoted to selling the idea that there was something missing in every monkey, and only by acquiring this 'missing piece' could they find happiness and fulfilment. Families who could afford it even began purchasing their own chains, believing it was the solution to their inferiority.

As time moved on, this way of thinking spread like wildfire, and today, we humans have taken the place of those monkeys. We've been wearing the chains of inferiority for generations, convinced that the two hands we were born with are not enough. We've come to believe that true happiness lies in gaining that imagined 'third arm,' the one that hangs like a chain around our necks.

Everyone who suffers from this feeling of inadequacy is searching for that missing piece, wandering through life trying to fill the void. This deep-seated belief has taken root in our minds—that if we don't achieve something specific in life, we will never earn respect or love. We've become a society where everyone is searching for their own chains, their own bondages.

But pause and ask yourself—why do we need these chains? Why do we seek out these bondages in life?

If your only goal is to chase money, then I must express my disappointment. You've been entrusted with a far greater responsibility—one that holds the power to carry your ideas forward long after you're gone. Every time your vision falters, remember, the very survival of your company is at risk. I often hear people say, 'I want to make money because I want to be the richest person in the world.' But ask yourself—why? Is it an influence you seek? Do you want to leave a lasting impact? And can you guarantee that this influence will preserve your company's success once you're no longer here?

No, you can't. A single signature, one misguided decision, is all it takes for a company to plummet from the peak of success to the depths of failure. Influence isn't built through the pursuit of wealth. True influence comes from ideas—ideas that leave a mark on the world, that improve lives, that inspire positive change. But when I see these lofty goals driven solely by a thirst for wealth, I recognise they stem more from desire and indulgence than from true dedication. Working solely for financial gain is a karmic bondage, a shackle that will hold you back from achieving real success.

If you want your company—your creation—to endure for generations, to maintain its impact in the market, you must make your actions and thoughts meaningful. They must be powerful, purposeful, and aligned with a higher vision.

In the chapters ahead, we'll explore how to make your ideas and actions truly effective. But for now, reflect on the karmic bonds that may exist in the growth of your company. You must define the boundaries and scope of these bonds, creating an ecosystem in which your creation can not only survive but thrive, generation after generation.

If you cannot release yourself from these karmic ties for the greater good of your company, or if you fail to outline the limits and purpose of these bonds, then I assure you— 'Your company is going to shut down.' It's up to you to decide how far you want your idea to reach. In life, we must discover a path where our actions are fuelled by resolve, carried out with love, and guided by unwavering faith.

This is the foundation of lasting success.

4

Mindfulness: Awake, Aware, Alive

———•———

'THE ONLY WAY TO SUCCEED IN ANY BUSINESS IS BY becoming truly 'aware' of your actions. When you carry out any task with full consciousness and clarity, that task becomes your vehicle, carrying you along the path to success.'

This story goes back to Anubhav's childhood. There was an old man in his village, a solitary figure with no family, no friends, and no one to rely on. He lived entirely in his own world, detached from the worries of others, and seemingly indifferent to any care or concern. People said that he once owned a house and land in the village, but for as long as anyone could remember, he'd lived in a small hut perched on a hillock at the village's edge. As a result, everyone referred to him as 'Baba of the Hill'.

The hillock wasn't particularly tall, about 30 feet, but its steep incline made it nearly impossible to climb. It wasn't just the slope that kept people away—there were countless stories and rumours about the mysterious Baba that had circulated for generations. Some claimed he was over a thousand years old, while others believed him to be an incarnation of some mystical force. There were even whispers that he possessed demonic powers, which explained how he could easily scale the hill like it was nothing. These tales struck fear into the hearts of many, but not Anubhav. He was endlessly curious, fascinated by both the hill and the enigmatic figure who lived upon it.

Since much of the land surrounding the hillock was barren, the children of the village had made it their playground, and Anubhav was no exception. One summer afternoon, when the mango trees were heavy with buds, he and two of his friends devised a mischievous plan. There were mango trees scattered around the hill, but they were the subject of another sinister rumour—that Baba had cursed them, and anyone who dared to eat their fruit would meet with disaster. But as children often do, they were tempted by the very things they were told to avoid.

Anubhav and his friends decided to raid the trees, determined to collect some *tikoras* (unripe mangoes) and make a spicy snack with salt and chilies. The time was set for 2 o'clock in the afternoon, and they armed themselves with sticks, slingshots, and whatever else they could find. By the time they had spent half an hour under the blazing sun, they had managed to gather about ten or twelve *tikoras*. Exhausted, they sat beneath the shade of a tree, ready to turn their loot into a feast.

They unpacked the essentials from their pockets—salt, chillies, spices, and even a makeshift leaf plate. But there was one critical thing they had forgotten: a knife. No blade, no sharp object to cut the mangoes. Their excitement quickly turned to frustration, which soon escalated into bickering. Arguments flared, and within moments, they were on the verge of pulling each other's hair out.

Suddenly, a raspy, trembling voice cut through their squabble: 'Get up, you little devils! Wake up!'

The voice was stern, sharp with disapproval. When the three boys turned around, they were struck with fear. From about 6-7 feet up on the hill, the Baba was swiftly descending towards them. His appearance was frightening—a long white beard, a skeletal frame, and a bamboo stick in his hand. The sight of him stunned the boys into silence, as if time had momentarily frozen. Then, with a swift leap from about three feet high, Baba landed on the ground. Anubhav was terrified. His two friends bolted, barefoot, screaming and yelling as they ran home. But Anubhav remained rooted in place, his body paralysed with fear. When he looked back, his friends were far gone, their shouts now barely a whisper on the wind. He just stood there, frozen, watching Baba approach slowly, inch by inch.

'What's your name, child?' Baba asked. Anubhav, though hesitant, answered. Baba then posed another question, 'You seem brave enough, tell me, would you climb this hill?' Anubhav shook his head indicating no, too frightened to speak. Baba smiled, amused by the boy's anxious expression, and said, 'You have the courage to stand your ground, but real bravery is climbing this hill. Only fighting other young kids like you won't make you brave.' With a voice full of nervous energy, Anubhav blurted out the entire story, his eyes brimming with tears. Baba listened attentively, and when he finished, the old man chuckled heartily. Reaching into his pocket, Baba pulled out a knife, flashing it before Anubhav. 'Come, sit with me,' he said, 'Let me help you make your *tikora bhujia*.'

Anubhav sat beside him, quietly observing as Baba peeled and sliced the mangoes. After some time, he summoned the courage to ask, in a timid voice, 'Baba, are you a beast?' Baba let out another loud laugh. 'Do you see horns on my head, boy? Or a tail with thorns? Look at me—do I resemble an animal to you?' Anubhav shook his head. His curiosity piqued, he ventured again, 'Then... Why do you live on this hill?' Baba's eyes softened, and with a solemn smile, he replied, 'At first, I came to this hill for a single reason—to conquer it. Day and night, I thought of nothing else but reaching the top.'

Baba continued, 'Days turned into years, seasons passed, but the peace and satisfaction I longed for never came. I chased it in everything, yet found nothing. One day, overwhelmed by the burdens of life, I decided I had enough. I thought this hill was the perfect place to end my suffering—it was high, rugged, unforgiving. I was ready to let go. You see, as long as I remained entangled in the world, I built my life based on the opinions and fears of others. I became a reflection of their limitations. What they feared, I feared. What they failed to do, I believed I could not accomplish either. My whole life, I thought, but never climbed. But on the day I decided to end it all, I had no thoughts—no fears, no desires. Success, failure, none of it mattered anymore. I only had one purpose: to reach the top. And on that day, without hesitation, I climbed the hill in a single attempt.'

Anubhav didn't understand everything the old man was saying, but his curiosity about climbing the hill had grown even stronger. Eagerly, he asked, 'Baba, will you teach me how to climb this hill?' Baba let out one final hearty laugh, stood up, and said, 'Here, your *tikora bhujia* is ready. Its tangy sweetness will wake you up.' He handed the food to Anubhav and began preparing to climb the hill once more. Anubhav, not ready to let go, ran a few steps after him and pleaded, 'But Baba, please tell me the secret to climbing this hill!' This time, Baba turned around, his voice loud and stern, 'You fool! How many times must I tell you? 'Wake up!' If you want to reach the top of this hill, wake up! Whatever you do, do it while fully awake.'

We all build our own mountains and hills in life, believing that peace and fulfilment await us only at the peak. As we navigate life's smaller and larger ascents, we cling to the notion that happiness is somewhere out there — beyond the next challenge, at the top of the next climb. But the truth is, peace and satisfaction aren't found at the summit. People venture to the Himalayas in search of serenity, but how many truly find it? Peace is not an external treasure; it is an inner state of being. You could be showered with all the wealth and fame in the world, but still, you'd have to look within to find peace.

People flock to the Himalayas, yet their minds remain shackled to their homes. The clouds above may reach out to embrace them, but they're fixated on social media, hungry for validation from strangers. I recently read a report stating that 60 per cent of people travel primarily to display their lives online, to impress others. Ironically, the very thing they're running from—the pressures and distractions of life—they carry along with them. While the snow of the Himalayas numbs their feet, their hearts burn with unresolved anger. Nature may be magnificent all around, but the mind remains tainted by personal conflicts. So, can peace really be found at the top of any mountain? Absolutely not. Those who believe peace is somewhere outside themselves are mistaken.

Anubhav's life had come full circle and led him back to Bangalore. In the last three years, he had made a name for himself in sales, but now he was restless, seeking a new direction. The desire to carve out something of his own, to pursue his own dreams, was growing stronger with each passing day. He often left home with an empty stomach, yet the hunger to achieve something greater fed his every need. Wherever he went, whatever he did, he kept his purpose clear and his motivation alive. Day or night, he pushed himself—learning, evolving, improving his skills and his character. What he didn't know, he taught himself. Each new target sharpened his abilities further, inching him closer to the man he wanted to become.

Anubhav had a point to prove—not to the world, but to himself. He knew he possessed something far more valuable than the superficial chains that bound him to the expectations of others. He had to grow, to break free from every limitation. Those chains—be they societal norms, professional roles, or the voices that said, 'Do this, don't do that; become a machine, manage but remain a slave'—rang in his ears every day. And every night, he vowed to tear them apart, piece by piece, because he refused to be defined by anything other than his own purpose and dreams.

'Man is often enslaved by his thoughts. Many times, the chains of these thoughts are so subtly woven into our consciousness that we fail to recognise their hold over us. But the beauty of the human mind is that these chains can be melted away by the power of our own awareness and consciousness.'

Anubhav's life was evolving, and so was his family. His daughter was growing up quickly, and no matter where he was or what he was doing, her future was always at the forefront of his mind. He was determined that the chains which had weighed him down for so long would not be passed on to her as an unwanted inheritance. He knew he needed to break free, and he even knew how to do it. But one truth was clear to him: before he could leap forward, he had to strengthen himself internally. He wasn't ready just yet.

Success in life comes not merely from action but from the ability to make the right decisions at the right time. And decisions aren't just simple choices between 'yes' and 'no.' Every decision is a reflection of your skill, your capacity to understand yourself and your surroundings. It's a test of how attuned you are to your emotional and mental state. It measures your wisdom, your awareness, and your intelligence.

One day, the office was abuzz with talk about Anubhav. He had doubled his sales target, a remarkable achievement. Anubhav was ecstatic. Everyone wanted to know his secret, the magic behind his extraordinary success. His boss summoned him to the cabin, showering him with compliments and making him feel indispensable. He was praised lavishly, shown dazzling dreams of an even brighter future. He was told he was just inches away from greatness, and if he could reach it, the very chains that held him back could be painted in beautiful colours.

The words of praise echoed beyond the office, reaching his family and filling the house with joy and celebration. The cabin overflowed with laughter, though some of it felt superficial. But then, in the midst of the congratulatory haze, a fleeting image of his daughter crossed Anubhav's mind. In that instant, all colour drained from his face. The promises and flattery, the artificial high he had been riding, all came crashing down. His daughter's laughter, innocent and pure, jolted him back to reality, and he was brought back to earth with a thud.

The boss noticed the change in Anubhav's demeanour, sensing his inner turmoil. But in that moment, Anubhav knew: no amount of praise, no dream, no colourful chain could replace the true freedom he sought—not just for himself, but for his daughter.

The boss placed a hand on Anubhav's shoulder, sensing something amiss. 'What's going on? Is everything okay?' he asked gently. Anubhav stood in silence for a moment, collecting his thoughts before speaking cautiously. 'Sir, I've never asked for anything before. But... if it's possible, could my salary be increased? Just by a couple of thousand rupees, not much... maybe two or three thousand...'

Before he could finish, the boss interrupted with a dismissive wave. 'Come on, young man, a person should only ask for what they deserve. You're worth millions—talking about a few thousand doesn't suit you. I think you need a break. Take a trip to Goa this week. We have a client there; you can meet with him too. Just land this Goa deal, and I promise, your promotion is a sure thing. And take your family along—you deserve to celebrate.'

Anubhav returned home quietly, unsure whether to feel happy or disappointed. His mind was conflicted. The idea of breaking free from these 'colourful chains' was gnawing at him, but he remained silent. There was an urge to cry, to let out the frustration building within him, but he feared that giving in to his emotions would only tighten the chains that bound him further.

Once in Goa, he watched his family laugh and enjoy themselves. But even in their joy, he couldn't shake the feeling of being shackled, unable to dance or sing with them. He couldn't bring himself to explain to his daughter that the price of these fleeting moments of happiness was his own sense of captivity.

Anubhav's life, wrapped in the chains of corporate success, was passing under the weight of tension. When he first moved to Bangalore, he believed that a salary of 40,000 rupees would be enough to live peacefully. But it wasn't. He then set his sights on earning 60,000 rupees, convinced that this would bring him contentment. After months of tireless effort, he reached that point, only to find the same restlessness lingering.

He thought, 'Maybe if I earn 85,000, things will finally settle down.' Two years later, he achieved that goal as well, but still, peace eluded him. With each increase in salary came a corresponding rise in needs, and with each new need came more expenses. Despite his growing wealth, the inner peace and satisfaction he had been chasing were nowhere to be found, not in the heights of fame, title, or money.

One day, Anubhav sat at his desk, disappointed, calculating the equations of his life. He was reflecting on which peak he could possibly scale to find peace. Then, as if carried by a gust of wind, the words of the Baba from the hill he had visited years ago echoed in his mind: *'Wake up, if you want to reach the peak, wake up.'* For a moment, Anubhav felt as though Baba was calling out to him. Stirred by this thought, he decided to take a few days off from work and head back home.

Upon reaching home, Anubhav's first destination was the hill. Standing at its base, he made a solemn vow to himself that he would climb it. At first, a wave of fear washed over him — *What if I slip? What if there's danger at the top?* — and he wondered whether the Baba would still be there, waiting. But he set these thoughts aside and fixed his mind on the task. He set his first goal: to climb 10 feet.

From that moment, his focus sharpened. He understood the weight of each decision — one wrong step could cost him dearly. So, with heightened awareness, he began his ascent, step by cautious step. To his surprise, he noticed signs carved into the rocks — likely footprints left behind by the Baba during his own journeys. Anubhav carefully followed these markers, studying each stone with intention, touching them as he progressed. His thoughts narrowed to the singular task of climbing, fully immersed in the moment. With this mindfulness, he ascended the hill much faster than he anticipated.

In that moment of reaching the summit, Anubhav finally grasped the deeper meaning of the Baba's words: *'If you want to reach the peak, wake up.'* He realised that consciousness — true awareness — was the key. It wasn't about rushing toward success; it was about the quality he infused into each action along the way. To be truly aware is to be awake — to be conscious of both thoughts and actions. This is the first door to success.

We often talk about brand awareness. But what is brand awareness, really? It's nothing more than a conscious effort to maintain the consistency, quality, and reliability of a product. It's not a separate, burdensome task. It's not like preparing a financial report while trying to drive a car — you don't have to choose one over the other. Awareness doesn't create obstacles.

If you're consciously riding a scooter, that act of driving becomes your meditation. If you're consciously coding a website, then that task transforms into a meditative practice as well.

Awareness, in its simplest form, means keeping your focus anchored to the task at hand. When you're working on a financial report, your attention should stay fixed on that report alone. If your mind drifts elsewhere — thinking about home while you're supposed to be focused on work — that's a state of unconsciousness. You can perform tasks in both a conscious and unconscious state, but awareness is not about merely having your eyes open; it's about being fully present. If you're at the office, but your thoughts are at home, you're not truly present in either place. In such a case, the work you're doing is being done unconsciously, because your body is at the desk, but your mind isn't.

Now, in the context of business, staying conscious is crucial. The business world is full of competing ideas and thoughts that constantly swirl around you. As a leader, you are surrounded by countless concepts, projects, and plans, all vying for your attention. But if you chase after them without focus, without conscious awareness, they will slip through your fingers like soap bubbles. You'll find yourself facing temptations that promise grand results: *If I do this, I'll achieve that, and if I pursue this idea, I'll get here.* As a founder, you're in a position that naturally attracts both positive and negative energy, creating a storm of ideas around you. But these ideas will only dissolve into nothingness if you lose your focus.

To stay aligned with your vision, it's essential not to be swept away by every fleeting thought or tempting opportunity. The real challenge is to remain steadfast on your path, avoiding distractions that could steer you off course. Being aware means filtering out the noise and focusing on the ideas and strategies that will drive your company forward. It's about resisting the pull of thoughts that could divert you from your ultimate purpose.

Once, Buddha was camping near a small town for a few days. One afternoon, a troubled disciple came running to him, visibly anxious. Buddha, noticing his distress, gently asked, 'What troubles you?'

The disciple replied, 'Master, I am utterly confused. Yesterday, while I was out begging for alms in the town, a strange thing happened. As I walked, a fleeting thought crossed my mind: *If I receive kheer today, I would be so happy.* No sooner had I thought this than a woman's voice called from a nearby house, 'Bhikshu, please come, I've prepared delicious kheer.' I was amazed at this coincidence. Grateful, I sat down and tasted the kheer—it was exquisite. But then, another thought slipped into my mind: *How wonderful it would be to have a second bowl.* Amazingly, before I could even finish that thought, the woman said, 'Don't worry, I have plenty of kheer. You may have another bowl.' I was stunned by the synchronicity and asked the woman if she could read minds. It turned out she was a devoted seeker, a sadhak, who had mastered the art of silence. Through her deep practice, she had developed the ability to hear the silence of others' thoughts. I bowed to her in respect and left, feeling blessed.

'But on my way back,' the disciple continued, 'a troubling thought arose: *Had I taken advantage of this woman's powers? Was I wrong to desire more?* This thought weighed heavily on me, and I resolved never to return to that town for alms.'

Buddha listened intently and then calmly replied, 'Do not be troubled. Follow my guidance, and you will find clarity. Go back to the same town, to the same woman's house, but this time, when food is placed before you, focus solely on the food. Be mindful of each bite—taste every grain with full awareness.'

The disciple did as instructed. The next day, he returned to the same house. The woman welcomed him again and served him food. But this time, the monk was fully present, his entire attention on the meal before him. Each bite was taken with consciousness—he savoured the texture, the flavour, the act of eating itself. As he ate, the monk noticed something curious: this wasn't kheer made from cow's milk at all. Slowly, it dawned on him that the kheer was made from the juice of a special fruit, not milk.

In that moment, he realised a profound truth: *When you are unconscious, the truth eludes you. Illusion and ignorance take root, and falsehood begins to feel like reality.* The more unaware you are, the easier it is to mistake illusions for truth and to form misguided beliefs. Consciousness, on the other hand, sharpens perception, allowing you to see clearly and act wisely.

The monk silently bowed in reverence to the woman and left, walking mindfully, this time in full awareness.

The essence of this story is simple: focus entirely on the task at hand. If you're eating, concentrate only on the act of eating, nothing else. Even 'doing nothing' can be a form of mindfulness, because what remains in that state is your pure presence—this is mindfulness. Eating, when done with full attention, becomes a mindful act because there's no other distraction. This is crucial to understand. Imagine Buddha expects that his disciples while eating, chant 'Buddha-Buddha.' But eating and chanting are two different activities. If you're chanting, you're not fully tasting the food, and if you're focused on the food, you cannot fully chant. By simply concentrating on the act of eating, the experience itself becomes conscious and meaningful.

Mindfulness makes everything more meaningful. When you're fully present in your work, the value of what you're doing increases. It's only with awareness that you can discern which decisions serve a company's purpose and which are distractions. No business can thrive without a clear understanding of which ideas are productive and which are irrelevant to its goals.

There are many misconceptions about mindfulness. People often think of consciousness or meditation as just another task on their to-do list. I often hear friends say, 'Life is so hectic, I don't have time to meditate,' or 'I was so busy with work today that I couldn't meditate.' But meditation isn't a task to complete; it doesn't require extra time. Rather, mindfulness is about bringing conscious attention to whatever you're already doing. If you're working in the office, let that task become your meditation. If you're walking, make that walk your meditation. When you walk, focus on the act of walking. Yes, thoughts will come, distractions will pull you away, but when you realise this, gently bring your focus back. This isn't a hindrance—it's the practice of mindfulness itself. The more conscious you are, the better you'll perform, because careful attention always improves the quality of the work.

The efficiency and skill with which you do any task depend on your level of attention. When you perform a task mindfully, your efficiency and competence naturally grow, as does your capacity to work. Not only that, but by working with full attention, the quantity of work you can accomplish increases, and you feel less fatigued. Fatigue often stems from the tension of being physically present in one place while mentally somewhere else. For instance, if you're at home but your mind is consumed with office work, you'll feel exhausted even while relaxing.

Let's look at it another way. Take any sport you enjoy—mine is football. When I'm on the field, I'm fully immersed in the game, playing with total concentration and enjoyment. Playing a sport obviously requires energy, but despite this, I always feel refreshed afterward. This is the power of mindful engagement.

Sports require energy—no matter what you do, your body will expend energy. Yet, isn't it fascinating that after playing a game of cricket, you feel refreshed instead of exhausted? It's true for any sport or activity you love.

Whether it's flying kites with friends, running around with your children in the park, or spending time with your pet, these moments don't drain you—they energise you. In these activities, you're fully engaged, your mind is entirely present. The world seems to disappear, and if it were up to you, you could keep playing for hours on end. Now, imagine if that same game were given to you as a job. What if you were paid to play it daily, but it became just another task on your schedule? Suddenly, it wouldn't feel the same. You'd start to feel tired—this is stress. Because in work, the body may be present, but the mind often drifts elsewhere. In sports, your whole being is engaged; your attention is right there, fully in the moment.

Athletes often say, 'I really enjoyed my game today.' What they mean is, 'I did what I wanted, and I was fully present in doing it.' Between 'I did what I wanted' and 'the enjoyment of that' lies meditation. It's about filling the present moment with awareness.

Consider Sachin Tendulkar. Before a crucial match, someone might have warned him: 'Sachin, Australia has a strong bowling attack today. The pitch is in their favour, and they've set up five fielders on the off-side. They're going to try to force you into playing off-side drives.' But in that game, Sachin scored a century by focusing only on the leg-side, mastering his shots there. This is the essence of meditation. His attention was on what he was doing, how he was doing it, and whether he was doing it right. The act of simply observing yourself in action, watching your own thoughts and behaviour, is awareness. This awareness breeds skill, competence, and mastery.

Standing in this awareness—simply watching yourself and the world—creates a profound sense of clarity and connection. It turns existence into an expression of love and understanding. If this truth becomes your lived experience, there is nothing left to do. The path vanishes, and life flows naturally in a state of sweetness and celebration. Knowing what is happening in each moment—this is meditation. Recognising how things unfold and being present to them is awareness.

A beautiful story illustrates this point. In the court of King Vikramaditya, famed for his wisdom, bravery, and generosity, there was always a flurry of activity. The king was deeply compassionate, often disguising himself to move among the common people, understand their needs, and shape policies for their well-being. His love for justice was so renowned that it's said three goddesses appeared before him to honour his fairness. The people adored him, and the court was constantly filled with those seeking an audience with their beloved king.

Among the many visitors was a fakir (a holy hermit) who had been coming to the court for years. Each time he visited, he blessed the king and gave him a fruit. The king, grateful for the blessings, always accepted the fruit and kept it. This continued for years. One day, the king's curiosity got the better of him. 'O Sadhu Maharaj,' he said, 'I've watched you for a long time. Every day you come to me, bless me, and give me fruit. I appreciate the gesture, but you could give your blessing without a gift. Why do you always bring fruit? I am confused. Is there something you are trying to show me, or have I unknowingly committed some offence for which I need forgiveness?'

The sage smiled at the king's words and replied, 'No, king, do not trouble yourself with such thoughts. My only message to you is this: The answer to every question lies within us. We spend so much time searching outside for what we already have within.'

Reflecting on this, the king returned to his room where he had kept all the gifts he had received over the years. There was a pile of fruits among them. On a whim, the king decided to cut open one of the fruits, and to his astonishment, he found a precious gem inside. He quickly cut open the others, and in each one, he discovered jewels—diamonds and priceless treasures. The king smiled in realisation, and his ministers, equally astonished, exclaimed, 'What we thought were just ordinary fruits were, in fact, priceless diamonds all along.'

This story reminds us that what we seek is often already with us—we just need the awareness to see it.

The ministers realised their mistake. They had taken the sage's daily gift as a mere token of gratitude, missing its true significance. Overcome with guilt, they rushed to find the sage and fall at his feet. But the king stopped them, saying, 'Let it go, ministers. You won't meet him now. Opportunities don't come by chance. He has already left.' If the king had been truly aware from the beginning, he wouldn't have dismissed the fruits as mere rewards. The true gem is not the jewels hidden inside; it is consciousness itself. No matter how many material treasures one may accumulate, this gem—awareness—is beyond value.

In everything you do, this awareness is your greatest asset. Watching yourself and observing your actions, staying mindful—this is the essence of consciousness. In fact, your entire existence is a dance of awareness. The more conscious you are, the more present you become. The more present you are, the fresher your mind feels, and the better you can focus on your tasks. To fully concentrate on any task is to bring consciousness into it. It's as if you are standing back, joyfully observing yourself at work. There is no other path, no distractions—just you, fully engaged, doing the work and living it completely. As you do this, you elevate the task, and in return, it refines you. And through this, consciousness grows. It is a cycle of joyful, mindful effort.

That's why I say, if you are not mindful of your work, your responsibilities, your thoughts, your purpose, or the direction of your company's growth, then no matter how many talented individuals surround you—even an army of advisors and experts—it will be meaningless. If you cannot bring freshness and energy into your work, if you cannot feel connected to it, then you are not working with awareness.

Your work should feel like play. You should understand what stress is, recognise its causes, and know how to resolve it. When you approach tasks with this awareness, it helps you make decisions from a place of clarity. But if you still feel confusion in your mind, it means there are unanswered questions. And until those questions are resolved, your work will not feel like a game—it will feel like a burden.

When you discover the answers within yourself, your work becomes effortless. You carry an image of your work within you—a mental blueprint—and only you know how to bring it to life. When you are genuinely happy and mindful as you work, the task itself becomes a conscious act. But if you lack this awareness, then neither your work nor your company will reflect your true vision. Without consciousness guiding your decisions, *'your company will shut down.'*

5

Curiosity: Seek, Explore, Discover

———•———

IT IS ESSENTIAL TO HAVE AN INSATIABLE THIRST AND A SENSE of dissatisfaction in life. If you truly want to make your presence known in the marketplace, there must always be a burning flame of desire within you. Yet, when I observe many people, it feels as though that spark has dimmed. They seem to be merely existing, not living with purpose. They are trudging along, carrying the weight of their lives like a burden, with no clear direction, no ultimate destination in mind. They move through life without any real sense of meaning, purpose, or ambition. They seem devoid of that inner fire, that burning drive that compels one to reach for more, to strive for self-improvement, to reshape themselves into a better version.

Remember, success in business—and in life—cannot simply be handed to you. It cannot be forced upon you. Success requires a deep, inner hunger. Only when you possess that thirst will you begin to yearn for the ocean. And when the thirst is genuine, the path to quench it will inevitably reveal itself. Before embarking on the journey toward success, it is vital to ask yourself: is there a thirst within?

One of the primary reasons people fail is that they have learned to be too content. We have settled. We've come to believe that what we have is enough, that this is all life has to offer. The thirst has dried up. Those with jobs are content with their jobs, and those who have started businesses are satisfied with the status quo. We've resigned ourselves to the idea that our lives are 'set.' We call this contentment, but the truth is, such complacency breeds neither happiness nor peace. A person who is truly satisfied with what they have, who accepts the limits of their current life without question, can never experience real growth or progress.

People often look at the life of a CEO and imagine that it's easy. They see the house in a metro, the luxury car, the children attending prestigious international schools, and think, 'There's no more dissatisfaction there.' They believe they are content. But the reality is different. Ask yourself honestly: has that inner thirst been quenched? Despite achieving wealth, status, and recognition, is there true fulfilment? The answer is often no. Even as business leaders, deep down, there is always a persistent flame of dissatisfaction burning.

That flame is the desire to be something more. It is the restlessness that comes from searching for meaning, significance, and purpose—knowing that there is still so much more to achieve, so much more to become. We may have accomplished a lot, but we are still far from reaching the summit. There is always a peak higher than the one we stand on today, and it is this knowledge, this drive, that pushes us forward. True leaders are never fully content. They know they can rise above their current state, and they are driven by the constant desire to transcend their limitations.

Everyone is out in search of success in the marketplace. But true success in life cannot be attained unless you're dissatisfied with the way life is currently unfolding. It's not enough to be complacent; you need to feel a restless discontent with your circumstances. We all have the potential to soar far beyond where we stand today. But it's crucial to remember that much of our dissatisfaction is misplaced—it's focused on external things that ultimately hold no meaning. A person in a prestigious position yearns for an even higher one. Someone with great wealth craves more, forever running in a futile race to accumulate. This kind of dissatisfaction, tethered to material things, will never be satisfied. We are all chasing something, but often it is the kind of dissatisfaction that pulls us deeper into the illusions of the world.

Anubhav had come to realise, over time, that the things he had placed so much value on—his name, title, reputation, and identity—were all hollow. The success, fulfilment, and peace he sought could not be found in his current job. If he was honest with himself, the salary had become a kind of bait, a lure that had only bought him chains. These were not physical chains, but seductive ones that bound him from within, keeping him tethered to a life that dulled his spirit. The weight of these invisible bonds was so heavy that they suppressed his own thoughts and desires. Suppressing your thoughts—that's inertia, or more plainly, it's slavery. In truth, carrying out someone else's thoughts while ignoring your own is the deepest form of slavery.

At that moment in his life, Anubhav's job was filled with everything that was dragging him into the darkness of inertia. He was bound by the chains of comfort: a high salary, the allure of status, and the attraction of power. But all of it amounted to nothing more than a gilded cage. His thoughts, his ambitions, his purpose—they had all become stuck. It felt like his life had come to a standstill, and he could no longer see any new challenges or learning opportunities ahead. There was a burning sense that he was meant for something more, but the path he had chosen was a golden cage—lavish in its trappings, yet binding his feet from flying toward his true destination.

Through the years, Anubhav had honed his skills and become highly competent in his field. He understood the intricacies of sales, mastering the craft to the point that he believed anything could be sold. But there was one thing he could never sell—his own thirst. The deep, unrelenting thirst to be something more, to offer something greater. The desire to create employment for the misguided youth, to offer purpose to others. This inner thirst, this hunger to become something better, had become the one thing that could not be satisfied by external success.

This thirst is vital to everyone's life. It is the flame that gives meaning to our existence, the force that drives us to uncover our true purpose. Without it, life becomes a series of empty achievements. But with it, life gains clarity, direction, and a sense of fulfilment that no amount of material success can ever provide.

A person dissatisfied with external things develops ego, but one who feels internal dissatisfaction begins to understand the true meaning of their existence. This distinction is simple yet profound. As humans, we often find ourselves unhappy with the material aspects of life. Someone who owns a motorcycle longs for a car, believing it will bring fulfilment. The person living in a two-bedroom apartment dreams of a bungalow, convinced that a bigger home will deliver satisfaction. Yet, dissatisfaction with external possessions is insatiable. The more we chase after these things, the more it fuels our ego.

External dissatisfaction only nurtures a sense of superiority and attachment to the very things that bind us. It breeds an ego that clings to its own limitations, mistaking them for strengths. It becomes obsessed with emotions and attached to the chains that hold it back. Anubhav, however, was aware of the truth beneath this façade. He knew those chains could be broken. If he truly desired it, freedom was within reach. But real dissatisfaction doesn't mean fleeing from reality. In fact, we cannot escape it, no matter how hard we try.

Everyone is racing through life—whether it's the pursuit of status, wealth, or prestige. Most of us are running without knowing where we're going, convinced that satisfaction lies somewhere ahead. But when we set out to find fulfilment externally, life becomes nothing but an endless race. We have become so accustomed to this relentless pursuit that, even if we lose sight of our destination, we keep running. Eventually, we become so entangled in the race that by the time we confront reality, we have strayed far from our original purpose. We lose our way. And when we realise this, we attempt to change course, often too late.

Anubhav found himself lost in this distraction. His life felt off-course because he wasn't holding the steering wheel. Others were driving the car of his life. Reflecting on his journey, he realised that most of his decisions had been dictated by external forces. Whether it was preparing for civil services on his father's advice, chasing corporate success after being dazzled by the allure of big cities, or returning to his hometown to do business at the suggestion of friends—his choices had been shaped by others. When that business failed, he moved back to Bangalore to survive, dedicating himself to the goals and ambitions of others.

By the time he reached this stage, Anubhav's life looked enviable from the outside, but inside, he was miserable. He had been running all his life, seeking satisfaction and success in the external world, but never found the fulfilment he sought. He had tried to please others, constantly reshaping himself to fit the expectations of the outside world, only to be met with darkness.

Now, at this point in his journey, Anubhav understood that this race was futile. He realised that the answers he sought were not out there but within. True satisfaction would come only when he stopped running from himself and found a place of inner stability, where he no longer had to chase external validation. It was time for him to embark on an inward quest, one that would reveal the true meaning of his existence and provide the peace and fulfilment he had been seeking all along.

Inner dissatisfaction does not mean escaping from life's challenges. Instead, it urges us to seek the true meaning of our existence, which can lead to genuine happiness. Our abilities, capabilities, and thirst for fulfilment are all internal, yet we spend so much of our lives searching for satisfaction outside of ourselves. This external pursuit is futile, which is why it becomes essential at some point to ask: What is the purpose of our existence? What is the meaning behind our actions? Only when we understand our own significance can we find real success in life.

'Our search for meaning drives us to evolve, transforming how we navigate reality and overcome adversity. By embarking on this inner journey, we awaken to our true abilities and potential.'

Once, a multinational company announced a high-level job opening. The interview process was rigorous, spanning four stages designed to test not just education and professional qualifications, but also problem-solving skills, critical thinking, and creativity. Thousands of candidates applied, and after the four stages were completed, an unusual situation arose. Two candidates had scored exactly the same, making it difficult for the HR team to choose between them. Unsure of how to proceed, they escalated the matter to the company's owner, who decided to personally interview both candidates.

At the scheduled time, both applicants met with the owner for their final interview. Remarkably, the owner made his decision in just five minutes. The HR team, which had taken three to four days to assess the candidates, was stunned. How could the owner make such a quick decision when the team had struggled to choose between them? Curious, they approached the owner to ask how he had done it.

The owner explained, 'It wasn't difficult at all. I asked both of them the same question: 'How was your experience in your previous company?''

The first candidate responded confidently, 'I am highly active, have strong problem-solving skills, and am disciplined. I consistently meet my targets ahead of schedule. However, I found the environment at my previous company unsatisfactory. My colleagues often had issues with my work style, and I felt the overall work culture hindered my personal growth. That's why I'm seeking a new environment where I can thrive and contribute to mutual development.'

The owner smiled and said, 'I rejected him.'

The HR team was shocked. The candidate seemed perfectly capable and driven, so why had the owner turned him down? The owner continued, 'I asked the second candidate the same question, and his answer was simple: 'My experience was excellent. The people were supportive, always eager to learn and teach.''

'I chose him,' the owner said confidently. 'The first candidate, although talented, is someone who runs from adversity. He's unable to adapt or change himself when confronted with challenges. His complaints about his previous workplace reveal a tendency to blame his environment rather than work through obstacles. On the other hand, the second candidate demonstrated a willingness to grow and learn, regardless of the circumstances. He didn't see his workplace as a source of frustration but as an opportunity to improve. His adaptability, positive outlook, and ability to face challenges head-on are what set him apart.'

The owner concluded, 'In life, you cannot run from difficult situations. Success comes when you learn to adapt, grow, and evolve within your circumstances. True progress happens not by changing your surroundings, but by changing yourself in response to those surroundings. Only then can you rise to a higher level.'

Let this be a lesson: Do not flee from challenges. Instead, embrace them, adapt to them, and you will find yourself in a better, stronger position.

To achieve true success in one's professional journey, it is essential to undertake an inner search—a search that brings clarity to life's purpose and meaning. This search is not about external factors but about recognising your own significance, understanding your strengths and abilities, and cultivating the resilience needed to confront reality in the face of challenges.

Anubhav, at this stage in his journey, had realised that the path he was on was taking him in the wrong direction. The increasing pressures at work, a boss who seemed indifferent, and a growing lack of confidence in his future growth had all started to weigh on him. It was clear that if he wanted to find success and achieve his true purpose, he would have to carve out his own path. He often asked himself, 'What comes next?' Yet, despite his dissatisfaction, he was fully aware that quitting his job wasn't an option. His current circumstances didn't afford him the luxury of starting over. He had already switched jobs multiple times, chasing new opportunities, but none had fulfilled the deeper sense of purpose he sought. Anubhav longed to make an impact—specifically, he wanted to provide employment to youth from small towns and villages.

In his professional journey, Anubhav had come to realise that his strength lay in sales. Over the years, he had explored various facets of sales and honed his skills. He found his passion in the art of storytelling—the ability to sell not just a product, but a story. Whether it was about the product itself or about meeting the needs of the customer, Anubhav believed that a compelling story could make people feel valued. If you want to succeed in sales, you must be able to offer more than just a product—you must give the customer a part of your own story. Show them how the product can make a moment in their life special. Yet despite his experience, Anubhav felt he had nothing of his own to sell—no personal venture to pour his passion into.

Still, he was determined to change his situation. He knew that success wouldn't come by running away from his current reality. Escaping wasn't an option. Instead, he resolved to start something of his own alongside his job. Based on his experience and foresight, Anubhav realised that influencer marketing was an emerging trend with growing potential. This insight led him to establish his own influencer marketing company, laying the foundation for a new chapter in his life.

Often, the biggest challenges in life are internal—our fears, lack of confidence, indecision, or reluctance to take risks. Yet, we frequently seek solutions in the external world. These problems can only be confronted when a persistent question begins to rise within us: 'What comes next?' When this question starts to echo in your mind, it signals the time to act. This inner questioning sets you on the path of discovery—the kind of discovery that leads to truth, that deepens wisdom, and that sharpens your awareness of your own potential. It is through this search that you become sensitive to your own needs and aspirations, and it is through this search that you can finally quench your thirst for purpose and fulfilment.

Your company's longevity and survival depend on your ability to steer it with prudence. Discretion is the mental clarity and wisdom within you that helps distinguish between good and bad decisions. A company's strength in overcoming challenges is rooted in this discretion. Without it, a company is like a boat set adrift in the vast ocean of the marketplace, without a rudder to guide it. Your discretion serves as that rudder, capable of navigating through the storms and waves of the business world. As the founder of a company, it is essential to cultivate prudence to ensure its success and longevity.

The process of 'search' is what sharpens this discretion. When you constantly ask yourself, 'What's next?' your insight and wisdom toward your business deepen. To be prudent is to be in touch with the truth, to experience reality as it is. You must be clear about what's right and wrong for the growth of your company. With that clarity comes wisdom, and with wisdom comes the ability to make sound decisions that lead your business toward success.

This search is also critical because it heightens your sensitivity toward your company. Sensitivity is a quiet, deep awareness of your company's state. When you're sensitive, you become attuned to every aspect of your business, whether it's thriving or struggling. With this awareness, you can act decisively to lift your company out of challenges. A seeker of truth must also know how to accept reality. Ups and downs are inevitable in business, but your sensitivity will drive your dedication to your company. It fills you with a sense of purpose, motivating you to remain steadfast in the market, no matter the conditions.

But the important question is, *what are we searching for?* The answer is simple: we are searching for the thirst that led to the company's creation in the first place. This is the thirst that uncovers the potential of both the company and the market. But keep in mind—this thirst should not be driven by greed or convenience. If your drive comes from desires like wealth, luxury, or comfort, it will never be truly fulfilled. The real thirst is born out of purpose—the one that made you leave behind an easier path to build something meaningful. It's the thirst that has fuelled your hard work, day and night. It is deep within you, and often it reawakens unexpectedly, even when you seem to be heading in a different direction. Believe me, every person carries this thirst within them. The key is to search for it, and the moment you find it, the path to your goal becomes clear.

However, one crucial element must accompany this thirst: hope. Hope is essential to the journey. Where there is despair, there will only be more despair. A step taken in hopelessness leads to defeat. But when a person is filled with hope, they can move mountains—literally. Take Dashrath Manjhi, for example. His thirst was for a path through the mountains, and it was his hope that enabled him to split open that mountain. His unwavering belief in his ability to conquer that massive obstacle was his hope. And the determination that 'I won't stop until I've succeeded'—that is the resolution of Dashrath Manjhi.

If you want to succeed in business, you must marry your thirst with hope and resolute determination. Only then can you turn your vision into reality.

Sankalp means, 'I will not stop until I complete this task.' When you work with this conviction, you become a sadhak (seeker) dedicated to your mission. Do you think Dashrath Manjhi's determination came without struggles? Didn't his hands suffer from slipping tools? Didn't the scorching stones burn his feet? Wasn't he beaten down by the unforgiving weather? And as he faced that towering mountain, wasn't it as if it mocked his efforts? The challenges were endless, but so was his hope. It whispered to him, 'You're almost there—just don't give up.' That's why I say, we must find that deep thirst within ourselves, coupled with hope, that sustains us for a lifetime. When we do, the effort we invest in quenching that thirst transforms into something greater—like a prayer for the sadhak. No obstacle, no mountain, no problem will be able to stand in your way.

A successful leader is like a seeker, driven by purpose and a thirst for fulfilment. He strives not just for material gain, but for deeper objectives that guide his life. His sadhana (dedication) to his goals reveals new paths to success. Through consistent action, he becomes a karmayogi—someone who works not just for the sake of work but with purpose and awareness. To achieve true success, you too must become a karmayogi, not a workaholic. Work done mindlessly will only lead to frustration. You must work with intention—not merely because the market demands it, but because through this work, you will discover your own potential. When you align your efforts with your true purpose, you'll find clarity in your path. Then, your work will be filled with joy and meaning, and you'll move forward with unshakable focus.

You must search for what you are not yet. Who searches for something they already possess? The real journey is about seeking what lies ahead, what remains undiscovered. What you've already experienced are milestones and memories, but they belong to the past. You're not who you were yesterday—yesterday, you understood the market as B; today, you've reached Z. Tomorrow, you'll want to know even more, and only you can undertake that journey of discovery.

This action—the act of searching—only happens when you decide to take it. No one knows your work better than you do. No one else can do your work for you. That's why I say: the work gets done when you engage with it. It is only through action that you will discover yourself, that you will satisfy your curiosity, and that you will quench your thirst for success. So I say this with conviction: if you don't feel that burning curiosity to uncover your own potential and the potential of your company, if the question 'What next?' doesn't strike you repeatedly, then definitely *Your company is going to shut down.*'

6

From Spirituality to Leadership

———◆———

'KABIRA KHADA BAZAAR MEIN, LIYE LUKAATHI HAATH, JO GHAR
phunka aapno, chale hamare saath.'

The marketplace is a complex tapestry of raw reality,
where allegiances are fleeting, and no one truly belongs
to anyone else. In this arena, self-interest reigns supreme,
and values are bartered without hesitation or remorse. If
you want to witness the world in its most unvarnished
and unfiltered form, there is no better way than to open a
company or establish a shop in this bustling marketplace
and take a seat among the chaos. As you immerse yourself
in this environment, you'll quickly come to the stark
realisation that here, in this unrelenting space, people will
not think twice before auctioning off your principles for a
fleeting advantage. In the world of commerce, loyalty is a
currency that often depreciates, and if you lose your focus,
even for just a fleeting moment, the ruthless tides of the

market will mercilessly cast you aside, throwing you to the ground in the process.

Yet, despite this harsh and often unforgiving truth, Anubhav was resolutely prepared to embark on the arduous yet exhilarating journey that lay ahead of him, diving headfirst into the vast and tumultuous waters of the market. Anubhav had already taken his initial steps toward this ambitious goal by laying the foundation stone of his influencer marketing company while still holding down a steady job to support himself. However, he was acutely aware that the real challenges were only just beginning to unfold before him. As anyone familiar with the intricacies of the business world knows, a company requires a substantial amount of capital to flourish and grow, and Anubhav's personal resources were far from ample. He found himself in a perpetual state of vigilance, constantly on the lookout for opportunities that could provide the financial backing he needed to transform his dream into a fully functioning corporate structure.

At this juncture, his modest salary from his previous job barely covered the basic necessities required to launch his company. In its current state, his 'company' was little more than a sleek website, a digital facade that masked the deeper challenges he faced. His only real assets were his unyielding willpower and the burning flame of inner dissatisfaction that relentlessly drove him to seek something greater than what he currently had. This desire for more, for something better, was the fuel that propelled him forward into the uncertain waters of entrepreneurship.

Imagine the marketplace as a vast river, and the company you build as a fragile boat navigating its currents.

Starting a company in this environment is not particularly difficult—there are countless boats adrift in the river, all competing for space. Anyone with a little ambition can come along, register a business, and proclaim themselves a participant in the market. There is no shortage of opportunities to mimic someone else's model, adopt their structure, and launch your own vessel into the rushing waters. However, the market is as unpredictable as it is vast—a churning whirlpool of waves and uncertainties that can easily overwhelm the unprepared.

To survive the depths of this marketplace, a boat needs more than just a basic structure. It requires a skilled helmsman—a captain capable of guiding it through the inevitable storms that will arise. In this analogy, success in the market doesn't merely come from floating along with the current. It necessitates a certain sharpness of mind to see through the illusion of the market's enticing promises, the courage to steer your own ship against the tide, and the wisdom to recognise when to dismantle old structures that no longer serve you. This nuanced understanding is the very essence of the journey that Anubhav was about to undertake.

In this moment of reflection, the phrase 'Kabir stands in the market, holding a stick' resonates deeply. If I were to align this sentiment with Anubhav's journey, I would assert that Anubhav too has arrived in the marketplace, fully prepared, standing tall, ready to face whatever challenges and obstacles may come his way. He no longer concerns himself with whether he will successfully make it to the other side of this tumultuous river or whether he will sink beneath the waves. Instead, he understands the profound truth that he must be his own captain, the helmsman of this ship that he has named his company.

Anubhav must embody the spirit of that helmsman, someone who is capable of navigating the unpredictable waters and charting a course toward the other shore. 'With a stick in his hand'—but this is no ordinary stick. It is a torch, ignited with the flame of dissatisfaction. This flame not only represents his passion and drive but also illuminates the path to success that lies ahead of him. Fueled by the unwavering force of his will and determination, Anubhav is ready to tackle the challenges that the marketplace will throw his way. His journey is not merely about survival; it is about thriving in an environment where many falter, using the light of his inner flame to guide him through the darkest of waters.

'Kabir said, 'Whoever burns down his house, walk with me." This profound sentiment resonates deeply with Anubhav as he stands at a critical crossroads in his life, where his nascent company symbolizes not just a business endeavour but a vital testament to his credibility and commitment to change. He yearns to rise above the chains of dependency, the burdens of ego, and the temptations that plagued him during his previous jobs—those experiences that often felt more like shackles than stepping stones. Anubhav recognises that this moment represents his opportunity to carve out his own path, a chance to redefine his existence on his own terms. He is acutely aware that he no longer has to answer to anyone, no longer has to conform to the expectations set by others. However, he also understands that his company, in its current form, is still in its infancy—merely a tender seedling. Yet, within that seed lies the potential to grow into a robust tree, one that bears the fruits of his hard work, dedication, and visionary aspirations.

In those early, formative days, countless questions flooded his mind, each one more pressing than the last. How would he navigate the vast and unpredictable waters of the market entirely on his own? What direction should he take amidst the multitude of options available to him? Anubhav was acutely aware that no company thrives in isolation; it requires a network of support, collaboration, and shared vision. In this journey, there was no established guide to illuminate his path forward. Who would stand by him through the trials and tribulations? Who would help him bring this dream to fruition? Anubhav knew that a successful company requires a committed team, a group of individuals who not only share his vision but are willing to walk alongside him on this challenging journey. The words of Kabir echoed in his mind: 'Whoever burns down their house, walk with me.' To burn down their house means to sacrifice everything—to let go of ego, desires, and temptations that often lead people astray. Anubhav was not merely seeking employees; he was searching for like-minded individuals who could make similar sacrifices, who were ready to leave behind their comforts and security to join him on this journey toward something greater.

Anubhav dreamed of creating a company that transcended the traditional notion of a business; he envisioned it as a powerful vehicle for purpose and meaning in his life and the lives of others. He wanted to inspire and unite people from diverse backgrounds, guiding them toward a common goal that would elevate not just themselves but their communities as well. This company was not just a means for survival or profit; it was a way for Anubhav to leave a lasting legacy, to fulfil a deeper purpose by empowering and organizing individuals who, like him, were ready to burn down the old structures of complacency and mediocrity to create something entirely new and transformative.

The question of what true leadership is remains a pivotal inquiry in the realm of business and beyond. The answer to this question is deceptively simple, yet it is often misunderstood, leading to dire consequences for individuals and organisations alike. Whether it's a CEO at the helm of a multinational corporation, a manager overseeing a team, or a team leader guiding their group toward a shared objective, the fundamental role of a leader is to take responsibility for the people they guide and mentor. They are tasked with inspiring and motivating others to achieve a common purpose or goal that transcends individual aspirations. Because of the immense weight of this responsibility, leaders are frequently scrutinized for their actions, decisions, and strategies. Throughout history, there have been leaders who wielded power and amassed wealth, yet time has branded them as tyrants, dictators, or greedy individuals whose legacies are marred by their misdeeds. This reality underscores the importance of operating with sound principles and noble objectives; without these, the results can indeed be disastrous, both for the leader and those they are meant to serve.

A true leader leads by example, setting the tone for those they guide. They embody the values and principles they wish to instill in others, making them figures worth following. However, the contemporary reality often tells a different story. In many workplaces, the person occupying a leadership role—whether it's the boss, manager, or team leader—often becomes the most disliked individual in the organisation. This unfortunate dynamic can arise when leaders fall into the trap of believing that 'if people don't like me, it means I'm doing my job right,' or they comfort themselves with the thought that 'the work must continue, regardless of what others think.' If your image in the workplace is that of an angry, domineering, or self-serving person who belittles others to boost your own ego, there will undoubtedly be negative repercussions. Such behaviour mirrors that of a dictator, someone who seeks to impose their will on others in order to achieve personal ambitions at the expense of their team.

The role of a leader should more closely resemble that of a coach or a teacher. Ask yourself: from which type of teacher would you prefer to learn? Would you choose the one who metes out harsh punishment for mistakes, or the one who corrects you with patience and wisdom? Too often, people misunderstand leadership, thinking it is fear or manipulation. They mistakenly believe that true leadership is about asserting authority over others through intimidation or coercion. This misguided approach transforms leaders into tyrants—whether through the threat of financial insecurity or by tempting people with money, titles, and prestige. Such leaders operate under the illusion that they can compel people into action through fear or bribery.

The first thing we must understand is that leadership is not about power, control, or domination. Leadership is the art of guiding others to accomplish tasks that align with a shared vision and collective goals. It's fundamentally about influence, not force; inspiration, not fear. When leadership is done correctly, it builds respect, trust, and collaboration, which in turn fosters lasting success for individuals and organisations alike.

Building a successful company, inspiring people from diverse backgrounds toward a common goal, and ensuring its longevity is the dream of every entrepreneur. Every founder aspires for their company to thrive for generations, leaving a mark on the world that transcends their own lifetime. In today's dynamic world, where industrial expansion and advancements in information technology are creating countless new opportunities, it has become easier than ever for individuals to introduce their innovative ideas into the market. This surge in creativity and entrepreneurial spirit is why we see an explosion of startups in various industries. The innovation revolution has unlocked the marketplace, allowing every idea, product, and concept to find appreciation and acknowledgment. However, when it comes to leading a company and confronting the harsh realities of the market, a growing number of companies falter and crumble because they fail to adapt and navigate the challenges effectively. Those that cannot steer their ships through turbulent waters, learn from their mistakes, and evolve with the changing landscape will inevitably find themselves lost amid the competition, becoming mere footnotes in the annals of business history.

In this era, everyone wants to rise above the crowd and lead it. However, many who lack self-discipline and awareness aspire to lead others, and such individuals and companies often falter when confronted with the realities of the market. If you are a CEO or in any leadership position today, your goal is to get people to follow your vision, align with your plans, and accomplish the tasks you set before them. But this cannot be achieved through coercion or fear. If you seek to be a successful leader, you must understand that effective leadership cannot rely on intimidation or force. You cannot inspire greatness in others by belittling or making them feel small.

A successful leader leads by example, not by force, but by inspiring and offering clear, logical guidance. Such a leader's success is rooted in spiritual qualities—truthfulness, kindness, love, courage, self-restraint, empathy, and cooperation. These qualities are not only essential for any leader; they are intrinsic to our humanity. They have always existed within us. If you can recognise and embrace these qualities, I can confidently say that you are tapping into your spiritual potential. Leadership grounded in spirituality is authentic, and only when you lead from this place can you become a truly successful leader. No matter what position you hold, if you lead by wielding authority through intimidation, manipulation, or diminishing the dignity of those around you, you not only undermine your team but also dishonour the position you occupy.

So, the question arises: How is spirituality relevant to business leadership? First, let me clarify that today's business culture is rife with misconceptions about spirituality. At the mere mention of the word, people often form preconceived notions or jump to conclusions. The more people you speak with, the more misunderstandings you encounter. One of the greatest misconceptions is that spirituality is tied to religion, but it's not about adhering to any external belief system. Rather, spirituality is about understanding an internal dimension—recognising the inner strength within each of us. It's about internal awareness, not external acceptance. It's about tapping into the power that resides in every individual, an inner sense of connection to oneself. And the person who understands and cultivates this inner power will inevitably find success in the external world as well.

In essence, to become a successful leader, you must first cultivate spiritual awareness. Only then will you be able to inspire others, build a lasting legacy, and face the ever-changing landscape of the market with resilience and grace.

A successful leader embodies a profound awakening from within, leading a life infused with clear purpose and meaningful direction. Such leaders possess a unique ability to assess situations with remarkable precision, employing their sharp perception and deep wisdom. They are not only visionaries with grand ideas for the future but also exhibit patience and composure, continuously seeking opportunities to transform challenges into advantageous situations. Courageous and highly skilled, these leaders hold the capacity to enact meaningful change that resonates throughout their organisations and beyond. At the very heart of their success lies a solid foundation built on altruistic love, empathy, and genuine cooperation. When a leader—whether they hold the title of CEO or manage a team—achieves spiritual awakening, their internal success manifests in these admirable qualities with remarkable ease. Once this inner success is attained, the manifestation of external success follows almost effortlessly.

Spirituality, at its core, revolves around mastering the art of internal control. It is only when an individual has gained mastery over their inner world that they can effectively navigate the myriad challenges that arise in the external world. This is precisely why I firmly believe that internal control is essential for any level of leadership. If you cannot lead yourself—if you cannot harness your own thoughts, emotions, and behaviours—how can you expect to lead others effectively? The ability to control the inner dimension of your being is synonymous with embracing spirituality. A person devoid of internal discipline leads a life fraught with misdirection and lack of purpose, ultimately resulting in an unfortunate existence. Until you take the time to understand yourself on a deeper, more profound level, you cannot uncover the true meaning of your existence. Without this essential self-awareness, your life will likely be dictated by the relentless pursuit of money, status, and fleeting material pleasures. External influences will overwhelm your decision-making process, and the trajectory of your life will become nothing more than a reaction to external circumstances. Thus, it becomes crucial to recognise your own inner aspirations and align them with a higher purpose—one that brings genuine meaning and fulfilment to your life.

A life devoid of clear purpose is, quite frankly, a disaster waiting to unfold. Whether it involves an individual or an organisation, without a defined purpose, you will remain directionless, unable to reach any meaningful destination. Imagine setting off on a journey without knowing where you're headed; eventually, that aimless wandering will lead to nothing but disappointment and distraction. The true joy of any journey isn't merely about passing through various milestones; it lies in arriving at a meaningful destination that resonates with your innermost desires and aspirations.

Spirituality serves as the key to truly understanding your existence and uncovering your life's purpose. It is only through this inner awareness that you can effectively discern your deeper aspirations from your external ambitions. The moment you stop chasing external achievements and start listening to the internal desire to become something greater, your life's purpose will gradually reveal itself. From that pivotal moment onward, you will be equipped to guide your company with clarity, ensuring that both your personal purpose and the organisation's goals align harmoniously. This alignment is why I firmly believe that, as a leader, you can only reach the pinnacle of success when your life's purpose is clearly defined and deeply understood.

Human beings exist in two distinct dimensions—the inner and the outer. The outer dimension, predominantly driven by ambition, is insatiable in nature. It constantly pushes you to envision achieving even more. For instance, today, you might hold the position of a teacher; tomorrow, you might aspire to become a principal. Today, you may find yourself in a managerial role; the next day, you could be dreaming of becoming a CEO. You might possess a house today, but tomorrow, you'll yearn for an island. Regardless of how much you achieve, the thirst for external ambition can never truly be quenched. You could conquer the entire world, and I can guarantee that your next ambition would be to set your sights on the stars. This insatiable nature of external ambition is precisely why I emphasise the importance of having a purpose in life—something profound and significant, something that bestows meaning upon your existence. It must be a goal that transcends the mere pursuit of wealth, status, or security, for those pursuits alone will ultimately leave you feeling unfulfilled and yearning for more.

This is precisely why spiritual leadership holds such critical importance in today's business culture. A great leader is one whose ability to experience life transcends physical limitations. Our bodies and minds, which represent the external dimensions of our being, are inherently finite and subject to various constraints. The body, for instance, is simply a product of what we consume and how we care for ourselves. The mind, on the other hand, is a complex collection of impressions and memories that we accumulate through our sensory experiences. A true leader, however, rises above these limitations. They become individuals who transcend their personal ambitions, leading with a vision that is greater than themselves—one that encompasses the greater good for their team and organisation.

If you operate solely at the physical or intellectual level, your leadership will inevitably be weak, confined by the past and the fantasies of the future. You will find yourself expending energy trying to compensate for the shortcomings that your body and mind have accumulated, constructing castles in the air instead of exploring new, meaningful possibilities. The essence of spiritual leadership lies in the ability to look beyond the immediate and the tangible, to grasp the profound interconnectedness of all things, and to lead with an authentic purpose that inspires others to engage in a shared journey of growth and achievement. Ultimately, spiritual leadership is about nurturing an environment where individuals are empowered to reach their full potential while contributing to a collective mission that reflects their shared values and aspirations.

People are drawn to leaders who break free from the repetition of the past. They want someone who can create and envision something that others can't even begin to imagine. A great leader sees beyond the constraints of past experiences and fleeting desires—something unseen by the rest. But this kind of leadership is only possible when there is a spiritual depth present within. Without it, no matter the field—be it business, politics, or any other—any leader lacking spiritual insight will find themselves limited and ultimately powerless.

A great leader possesses the ability to organise and steer situations and challenges in alignment with the company's goals. However, you can only influence external circumstances when you first have control over yourself. True resilience in the face of external challenges comes from mastering your inner world.

One key insight to grasp in the journey of leadership and personal growth is that no human being, regardless of their status, wealth, knowledge, or power, can ever attain complete control over external circumstances. The reality we face is that we cannot dictate every outcome, nor can we ensure that everything unfolds according to our meticulously crafted plans. This fundamental truth is precisely why, without a deep sense of spiritual awareness, most people find their lives dominated by external forces and influences. It's a trap that many of us continuously fall into, harbouring the expectation that the world will conform to our desires and align with our visions. However, the harsh truth remains: no matter how well you plan or strategize, it is unrealistic to expect the world, or anyone in it, to behave exactly as you wish or hope.

The vital takeaway from this realisation is that while we cannot control external circumstances, we can, at the very least, learn to manage our own reactions and actions as we see fit. This is where the essence of personal mastery comes into play. Now, take a moment to imagine this empowering scenario: if you possessed the ability to control your inner state with precision—shaping it exactly the way you wanted—how would you choose to feel? Undoubtedly, your instinct would be to maintain yourself in a state of happiness and peace, free from the burdens of stress, sadness, anger, or any other negative emotions that might cloud your judgement. Unfortunately, the reality for many individuals is that they suffer immensely because they allow their internal states—emotions, energies, and capabilities— to be shaped and dictated by external circumstances that are often beyond their control.

This dynamic is particularly evident in the realm of leadership. Leaders and organisations that lack self-control and the ability to manage their inner states are the ones that crumble when faced with external challenges. When we discuss failure or breakdowns within teams or companies, we often trace these issues back to a fundamental lack of awareness and acceptance of reality. It is essential to understand that no matter how meticulously you plan or prepare, new challenges will always arise, and problems will inevitably occur along the way. This is simply the nature of our present reality, filled with unpredictability and constant change. These challenges cannot be sidestepped or ignored; they must be faced head-on and addressed directly. You can only tackle these challenges effectively when your inner state is firmly within your control and you have cultivated the emotional resilience to respond appropriately.

This is precisely why I assert that an ideal leader is someone who remains composed and centred in any situation, regardless of the external pressures they may encounter. Such a leader possesses the determination and fortitude to transform the circumstances they face, viewing every situation as a learning opportunity and an occasion to test their own abilities and inner strength. Instead of being reactive and allowing external challenges to dictate their emotional responses, a successful leader takes proactive steps to influence and shift external circumstances through their inner qualities. These qualities include vision, courage, restraint, dignity, humility, and discernment.

By embodying these traits, leaders can not only navigate the complexities of their environment but also inspire and uplift those around them. They understand that true leadership goes beyond merely managing tasks or directing others; it is about fostering a culture of growth and resilience, both within themselves and within their teams. In this way, they create a supportive environment where challenges are viewed not as obstacles but as stepping stones toward greater understanding and achievement. The journey of leadership, therefore, is not just about guiding others but also about mastering oneself and cultivating the inner strength necessary to thrive in the face of adversity. Ultimately, it is this inner mastery that enables leaders to respond to the unpredictability of life with grace, ensuring that they and their organisations not only survive but flourish in an ever-changing world.

But remember, these qualities are not developed by chance. They are the result of inner work—spiritual growth. True leadership begins by cultivating these qualities within oneself. Only by mastering the internal can you successfully navigate the external.

Vision

It is often said, 'If the mind gives up, defeat is inevitable; if the mind is steadfast, victory is assured.' This emphasises that true success begins from within. To put it more technically, whatever we achieve internally is what we strive to manifest in the external world. In simpler terms, we cannot attain external success until we first achieve it internally. However, this internal success is only possible when we possess the ability to perceive reality clearly and consciously. This ability, this power to see and understand the essence of things, is called *vision*. It is not merely about physical sight; rather, it is the inner awareness that continues observing, even with eyes closed—whether we are awake, asleep, or engaged in any activity. This vision is the spiritual core of a human being.

A successful leader is distinguished by this special quality—being a sharp visionary. He has the capability to foresee possibilities and opportunities even in challenging circumstances. It is this vision that awakens a person internally. To consciously see and understand the truth of time and circumstances is the essence of wisdom, the hallmark of an awakened mind. The moment we begin to perceive a problem clearly and consciously, the doors of possibility open, allowing us to change our circumstances. It is vital to remember that problems are first solved internally, which is why we must always begin by addressing them within ourselves. With courage and inner strength, success becomes attainable.

Courage

They say the world can be a frightening place, and the same is often said about business. It feels daunting because reality is full of uncertainties and mysteries. In business, we face new challenges and problems every day. No matter how much we plan or prepare, the present moment always seems to deliver a new issue to our doorstep. These problems seem overwhelming because we try to avoid them, constantly seeking an escape. But as I've often said, we cannot escape the present. One principle to live by is: *'Whenever reality or problems seem to crush you, do not view it as misfortune; instead, see it as an opportunity, for there is no greater fortune than to endure and emerge victorious.'*

A great leader reveals their true strength in those moments when circumstances are unfavourable, when life doesn't seem to align with their plans, when destiny appears to work against them. In these situations, the best-laid plans often falter, and the destination may seem out of reach. Yet, a true leader does not lament their fate. They summon the courage to face those circumstances head-on, declaring, 'I will not yield; I will not stop.' This power to stand firm against adversity is not external—it is an internal force. And that force is called *courage*.

Courage is the most fundamental quality of all successful leaders, and the most remarkable thing about it is that it cannot be faked. Whether it's the courage to embrace personal growth or step beyond the safety of your comfort zone, or the courage to take risks and stand by your convictions, courage is indispensable. It means standing up for what is right, speaking truth in the face of adversity, and rejecting what is wrong without hesitation. Courage is essential for making the right choices, even when they are difficult.

Whether it's the courage to unite people and lead them forward or the strength to stand alone when necessary; whether it's the bravery to attempt something challenging or make tough decisions, courage is the inner force that equips you to face every challenge head-on. It is this quality that empowers a leader to always act on what is right, regardless of the circumstances.

Self-control

'A leader's greatest strength lies in mastering the art of self-control.'

I've known many people who remain unfazed, regardless of external circumstances. Even when things are not in their favour, their response is calm and measured. No matter how tumultuous the storm around them, their demeanour is as serene as still water. It is nearly impossible to rattle such individuals or watch them crumble under pressure because they have mastered the control of their own minds.

The truth is, every person encounters complications in life—what we might call an internal *civil war*. This inner conflict arises because there is a burning desire within us for *something more*. We aspire to achieve, to rise, to become someone. But when reality presents its harsh challenges, when we find ourselves surrounded by difficulties, it is the power of self-control that fortifies us. It gives us the strength to face adversity head-on. This remarkable force of self-regulation is what we call *self-control*.

As human beings, we strive to extract the most from our finite lives. We dream of achieving great heights. If your company generates a revenue of ₹100 crores this year, next year the goal becomes ₹2000 crores. If today your business is in one city, tomorrow you envision its presence across the globe. But time—reality—is not in our control. Not everything can go according to plan. Often, our ambitions and passions drive us to such extremes that when setbacks occur, we falter and lose our balance due to a lack of self-control. When our nature and behaviour slip out of our grasp, we call it *losing our temper*. In this state, our reactions—whether physical or emotional—are beyond our control.

To be a successful leader, one must cultivate the power of self-mastery. This inner strength is called *self-control*. It is the force that keeps our impulses and energies harnessed within us, enabling us to lead ourselves with discipline. Once a person becomes the master of their own mind, no external challenge can topple them. This is why a disciplined leader remains steadfast, no matter how unfavourable the circumstances may be. Standing firm in the face of adversity, with self-restraint, reflects true determination. Self-control is the internal compass that aligns a leader towards their goals, no matter how difficult the journey.

If you examine the lives of any successful leaders, you'll find they were driven by intense passion—a burning desire to achieve something, to become someone. This passion is part of human nature. But when that passion lacks direction or self-control, the result is nothing but frustration and disappointment. The world, particularly the market, is filled with distractions—temptations and frustrations are everywhere. *If you achieve this, you'll get that; if you fail here, you'll miss out.* These endless enticements and fears cloud our vision. Therefore, it becomes vital to control the passion within us; otherwise, we risk becoming lost and distracted.

A person's passion can fuel their desires and dreams, but without proper restraint, this energy becomes untamed. Passion, left unchecked, can lead us astray. That is why we need the whip of *self-control*—a discipline that keeps us on course and prevents us from chasing empty ambitions. This whip of restraint keeps us from following the crowd mindlessly. When you study any remarkable leader, you'll see that beyond their passion, what sets them apart is their ability to harness their inner power. They did not seek to blend in with the masses. Instead, they embraced their imperfections and, through self-control, motivated themselves and those around them to become better, eventually leading them to success.

As a CEO or leader, you too likely experience a constant *civil war* within—an internal battle where your ambitions, desires, anger, and frustrations clash with the external demands of leadership. But a true leader rises above this inner conflict. You have the ability to channel your energy and passion to guide your company towards a positive direction. Whether your goal is to build a better society or contribute to national growth, we can only lay the foundation for a better world by transcending ego, selfishness, and unchecked ambition.

To lead a successful company, you must first be in control of yourself. You must resist the provocations of others, set aside selfish interests, and operate effectively under immense pressure. You must overcome your fears and physical limitations in order to serve others with excellence. We must think beyond the short-lived passion of the crowd, for only then can we and our companies truly succeed in this market. And this victory—this journey to success—must begin from within.

Dignity

'True peace comes when you stop caring about what others think or how they judge you.'

This isn't about disregarding people or their opinions—it's about protecting your *self-respect*, which is best described as *dignity*. Dignity is an inherent quality that defines our humanity. If I were to define it, I'd say, 'It's the belief that all human beings are equal and that their existence deserves to be valued and respected.'

Before we go any further, let's distinguish between dignity and respect. A common problem I see in many workplaces is that people often complain, 'I'm not getting the respect I deserve.' They get emotional, frustrated, or even angry over the perceived lack of respect. But is respect really so important that it must be demanded? Can it truly be desired, much less controlled?

Respect is something that lies outside of your control. One day, thousands may welcome you with open arms and flowers, but tomorrow, those same people could be throwing stones. Today, people may bow their heads in admiration, but tomorrow, they might be sharpening their knives. Respect is fleeting. But *dignity*—dignity is yours alone. It is internal, a reflection of your own values and self-worth. Respect is not a bad thing, of course—it's wonderful to receive, but since it is beyond your control, it's pointless to become upset over it. On the other hand, dignity is entirely within your control. No matter the external circumstances or the pressure you face, as long as you hold onto your dignity, no one can take it from you.

In the business world, it is crucial to maintain your values and preserve your dignity. Principles are non-negotiable. You cannot compromise your self-respect or integrity, no matter the situation. People may celebrate your success, cheer for you, and shower you with praise, but remember, the same crowd will ridicule and criticise you when you stumble. That's why it's essential to rise above the noise. As a CEO, as a leader, you must set a standard of conduct that reflects the values you live by. This standard is your dignity.

As a leader, your actions should always align with your dignity. It should never matter whether people are criticising you or praising you. Remember this: 'Success is not determined by what others think of you or their

opinions; it's determined by your integrity and dignity.'
While you can't stop people from talking about you, you
have complete control over how you respond to their words.

To be a successful leader, remind yourself constantly
that nothing is more important than your dignity and
integrity. Keep telling yourself, 'I am doing the right thing.'
Remind yourself that 'there is no greater fan or critic than
myself.' And if proof is needed, let yourself be the witness.
This is what great leaders do—they focus on doing what's
right, regardless of the circumstances, risks, or doubts. They
ignore the noise and push forward, driven by their own
values. Because the real satisfaction comes from doing what
is right, not from seeking validation.

Humility

'Leadership never allows one to declare, 'I am everything.'
The moment you start believing you're the best, flip through
the pages of history. You'll find countless figures time has
slowly erased.'

It is human nature to compare ourselves with others—
to measure where we stand. Whether it's the stranger next
to you on a journey or a colleague at work, our mind is
constantly calculating. We compare ourselves with those
we admire, as well as with those we envy or dislike. This
urge to prove ourselves superior to others is nothing more
than a boost to our ego. We nurture this ego, believing it
sets us apart, makes us better. And yet, the slightest bruise
to this ego causes pain. The mind aches. We feel offended
because we constantly seek validation, striving to impose
our opinions and influence.

But this internal battle, this need to win, is an endless and futile struggle. The truth is, no matter how vital you seem today, no matter how wealthy or powerful you become, time has no regard for your stature. History shows us that even the greatest will be forgotten.

Take the life of Alexander the Great, for example—a man who conquered vast lands and was immortalised by his accomplishments. Yet, in death, his grave stood side by side with his mule and the slave who carried his belongings. The earth took them both, without bias or distinction. The one who believed himself invincible met the same fate as his servant. Time does not spare anyone. In the end, it is time that triumphs.

In reality, none of us are special. We are as human as everyone else. Our physical bodies, our very existence, are limited. We cannot achieve everything within a single lifetime. The key is to embrace that we all hold equal significance in this world. Titles, prestige, fame, and power are fleeting; they will remain behind when we are gone. Nothing in this universe is permanent. If you doubt it, look at the ruins scattered around the world—remnants of civilizations where countless people once lived and were lost to time. Their names may be etched in stone, but today, they are little more than fading memories.

Accept your role in life. Evaluate yourself honestly, not by the world's standards, but through your own internal compass. Create an *internal scorecard*, where you can measure your principles, values, and abilities with sincerity. This isn't about diminishing yourself but rather recognising your limitations. Only by acknowledging your flaws can you grow, improve, and become a better version of yourself.

Life moves swiftly—joy and sorrow, success and failure, even our greatest achievements, are temporary. Who you are today may not be who you are tomorrow. Human existence is like a river, always flowing between the past and the future. Yet, instead of riding these waves, we often make the mistake of trying to measure the unfathomable depths of time, an abyss beyond our control.

To be a truly great leader, you must first conquer your ego. And that victory begins by making humility a habit. Humility isn't a sign of weakness; it's a sign of strength, wisdom, and self-awareness. It's the understanding that, in the grand scheme of life, we are all just fleeting travellers, bound by time. Only by letting go of the illusion of permanence can you truly rise as a leader—not above others, but alongside them.

Cooperation

I've said it many times—there is no escaping or fighting the present. Yet, we often exhaust ourselves trying to battle the challenges that life presents. Remember, you cannot overcome a problem by waging war against it. The moment you engage in a fight, the problem grows larger, more intimidating. Fear sets in, and suddenly, we're not battling the issue itself but rather our fear—fear of losing control, fear of failure, and fear born of our own imagination. But here's the truth: problems aren't solved by resistance. They are solved through cooperation.

Cooperation is the key to unlocking the best in yourself and in others. It is an indispensable quality of true leadership. Leadership, at its core, is the ability to create an environment where others can surpass their own limitations. When you lead effectively, people often achieve things they never thought possible. Why? Because they know they have a leader who walks beside them—someone who will stand with them, guide them if they stumble, and point them in the right direction if they lose their way.

Without a spirit of cooperation, leadership is powerless. Without it, we cannot bridge the gap between our needs and the needs of others. As you navigate your business journey, where people look to you as a leader, you will encounter those who are willing to give everything for you. Why? Because they believe in you. They trust that you will help them become something greater, that you will guide them to achieve things they could never accomplish alone. This is the art of aligning your purpose with the aspirations of others. And when you stand as a united team—when your leadership is infused with the power of cooperation—every person's contribution becomes invaluable. It strengthens your leadership and equips you to face any challenge, no matter how daunting.

It's often said that bad companies crumble in a crisis, good companies survive it, but great companies *thrive* in adversity. But this transformation, this elevation, begins within. It starts with you. If you want to lead successfully, you must first nurture and refine your own inner qualities. These spiritual attributes are the foundation of not only your leadership but of your entire organisation. They are the pillars upon which greatness is built. Without these qualities, no amount of external success will sustain your company, your leadership, or your legacy.

Leadership without cooperation, without a deep connection to one's purpose and the needs of others, is destined to fall. But leadership that embraces cooperation—that embodies the best in humanity—can overcome any obstacle and elevate everyone around it. That is the essence of true leadership. That is why I believe that for a leader to be truly successful, they must cultivate these inner, spiritual qualities. Without them, I can say with absolute certainty that 'Your company is going to shut down.'

7

Great Leaders Create Leaders

———•———

'LEADERSHIP IS NOT A DIVINE GIFT, NOR IS ANYONE BORN with it. It is a lifelong journey—a process of growth, learning, and refinement that unfolds with experience. In fact, it's fair to say that with the right mindset and moulding, anyone can develop into a leader.'

A great leader is driven by a powerful and compelling purpose, a vision that serves as a guiding light and fuels their every action. This purpose is not merely a fleeting notion or a passing fancy; it is a profound commitment that shapes their thoughts, decisions, and interactions. However, it is essential to recognise that no great purpose, dream, or goal can be realised in a single day, nor can it be achieved in isolation. The journey toward fulfilment is complex and often requires the combined efforts of many. Without the spirit of cooperation and collaboration, true success remains tantalisingly out of reach. To genuinely fulfil your purpose and achieve lasting success, you must continuously evolve and adapt as a leader, embracing the ever-changing landscape of challenges and opportunities that life presents.

Each day is a new opportunity, bringing with it fresh lessons, unique challenges, and critical decisions that shape not only your leadership journey but your life as a whole. Leadership is far more than simply making tough calls, drafting plans, or concentrating solely on personal growth. A successful leader understands that each day encapsulates an entire life in itself—a series of moments that should be approached with intention and meaning. They embrace every moment with a profound sense of responsibility and purpose, not just toward themselves but also toward those they lead. A true leader views life as a rich tapestry of opportunities, each one an invitation to lay the groundwork for a better future. Their vision allows them to see situations with clarity, anticipate challenges that may arise, and prepare themselves accordingly.

Possessing a relentless drive, a great leader seeks to understand new situations, confront emerging obstacles, and extract valuable lessons from every experience they encounter. They recognise that the world is constantly shifting, and as such, they must remain agile and responsive to the demands of the moment. A great leader is, at their core, a lifelong learner. They understand that success is not a static state; it requires continuous growth, adaptation, and resilience in the face of adversity. They exhibit fearlessness when confronted with risk, viewing uncertainty not as a threat but as a teacher imparting invaluable lessons. Rather than waiting passively for a miracle to occur or relying solely on luck, they actively seek to uncover insights in times of adversity, using those revelations to forge ahead with renewed vigour and determination.

True leadership is a constant process of learning, unlearning, and relearning—a dynamic and active state of being that demands engagement and introspection. A great leader does not rest on their laurels or become complacent due to yesterday's victories. Instead, they approach each day with renewed focus and purpose, always ready to adapt, grow, and inspire those around them to do the same. They understand that leadership is not merely about personal achievement but also about fostering an environment where others can thrive and reach their fullest potential.

A hallmark of any great leader is their remarkable ability to remain unfazed by the passage of time. They are neither caught off guard nor overwhelmed by surprises, worry, or excitement. Instead of ignoring challenges or postponing decisions, they confront them head-on with courage and conviction. As CEOs and leaders, we constantly devise new strategies, explore fresh avenues of business, and test our capabilities in diverse markets. Yet, like all human beings, we must acknowledge our limitations and the constraints that accompany our roles. We cannot do everything ourselves, and perhaps more crucially, we must recognise that time is not an infinite resource. The realities of old age and death are not distant uncertainties—they are inevitable truths that we must come to terms with.

We understand the value of time deeply and intimately. Our desire is not to remain stagnant; instead, we strive to push forward, constantly evolving and adapting to the changing landscape around us. The truth is that as CEOs and leaders, we aim to maximise every opportunity that the market presents, seeking to transcend the boundaries of time and circumstance. However, the passage of time itself is not within our control. The only way we can extend our reach beyond our years and ensure that our legacies endure is by planning for a future in which we are no longer present.

Consider this for a moment: you've poured your heart, soul, and energy into building this company, nurturing it with care, values, and a clear vision for its future. Yet, in a few decades, you may not even be around to witness its growth and evolution. The thought of who will take care of it, who will uphold those responsibilities when you're gone, can be unsettling and even distressing. What will become of the values and principles you spent a lifetime instilling in your organisation? Who will ensure that your vision continues to thrive and that the foundation you built remains strong in the years to come? These are the critical questions that every leader must grapple with, for they speak to the essence of true leadership: the ability to create a lasting impact that transcends one's own lifetime and continues to resonate through the actions of others long after you are gone.

Ultimately, a great leader understands that their role is not just to lead in the present but to cultivate a legacy that endures—a legacy rooted in purpose, collaboration, and a commitment to continuous growth and learning.

'As a CEO, my primary responsibility is to cultivate leaders at every level who can think beyond me, act decisively, and carry the torch forward.'

A successful leader is one who anticipates the future, making deliberate plans for their absence. They cultivate the next generation of leaders, equipping them to implement meaningful changes, make informed decisions, and achieve objectives even when the original leader is no longer present. These emerging leaders are entrusted with upholding the values and principles that guide the organisation, ensuring continuity even in the absence of direct feedback or oversight.

Every founder aspires for their values to resonate with customers, allowing individuals to connect their personal experiences with the products and services offered. A CEO desires their influence to endure in the marketplace, which is why they explore diverse business dimensions and remain open to change. Discussions about workplace culture, productivity, and effective management are commonplace; seminars and meetings are held to strategize how to achieve collective goals. While witnessing a leader actively engaged can motivate others to emulate their achievements, a pivotal question arises: what qualities make a leader's presence truly charismatic? What is it that inspires people to trust and follow their direction?

It's crucial to understand that leadership extends beyond merely creating a conducive environment or promoting cultural values. It is not solely tied to profit margins, influence, or prestige. The essence of leadership lies in enhancing the life experiences of followers, employees, and customers—both directly and indirectly.

In today's rapidly shifting business landscape, characterised by confusion and temptation, the call for authentic change is urgent. However, this transformation must be profound rather than superficial. A genuine workplace culture is not defined by amenities like pool tables or yoga rooms; rather, it is an environment where employees recognise their significance. An effective business culture fosters a space where individuals can appreciate their value without fear, empowering them to enhance their skills through self-discipline.

A capable leader views their employees not as a faceless crowd but as vital partners in achieving shared goals. They acknowledge and celebrate each person's unique skills and contributions, fostering motivation and preparing their team to embrace leadership roles in the future. This nurturing approach creates a legacy of leadership that transcends the leader's tenure, ensuring the organisation's values and mission endure long after they are gone.

In today's fast-paced culture, it is crucial for individuals to learn how to lead themselves effectively. The encouraging reality is that anyone can become a leader by recognising their unique abilities, assigning them a clear purpose, and equipping them to tackle various challenges. As we've explored in previous chapters, essential qualities of a capable leader include courage, restraint, dignity, humility, and cooperation. These traits are inherently human and can be cultivated through consistent practice. If we can provide this training within our workplaces, we can indeed transform employees into leaders, preparing them to face new challenges.

Imagine a workplace where employees are empowered to enhance their self-leadership skills, fully engage with the organisation's mission, and grasp the significance of their roles. In such an environment, a Spirituality Workspace becomes a vital link, enabling you to evolve your company into a motivated learning organisation—a model that embodies growth and transformation. This is a model that fosters leadership by connecting individuals to a shared purpose, thereby equipping them to carry on initiatives long after you have moved on.

'A workplace where individuals find meaning in their existence and derive satisfaction from their work embodies the essence of Workspace Spirituality.'

A significant portion of our lives is spent in the workplace, and at some point, it becomes our responsibility to seek meaning and fulfilment beyond mere life goals, money, status, and prestige. Research shows that workplaces where individuals are satisfied and committed see a marked improvement in productivity. It's important to understand that motivating someone to join your cause cannot be achieved solely through promotions or raises. True engagement comes when people feel a sense of belonging, as if they are part of a family united by shared objectives.

In today's dynamic and often competitive business landscape, cultivating a spiritual workplace can be instrumental in achieving remarkable and sustainable goals. A spiritual workplace goes beyond the traditional metrics of productivity and efficiency; it fosters personal and professional development, inspires authentic leadership, and unites individuals as a cohesive team dedicated to the company's overarching vision, goals, and culture. This innovative approach emphasizes valuing people as whole individuals, rather than merely as employees who clock in and out for their shifts. Often, in conventional work environments, we leave significant parts of ourselves at the office door—our passions, dreams, and aspirations. However, a spiritual workplace creates an environment where people feel comfortable, accepted, and fully engaged with the organisation's objectives, leading to higher morale and productivity.

To put it simply, a spiritual workplace embodies a rich and inclusive culture where individuals work collaboratively to bring the company's vision to life through cooperation, mutual respect, and shared values. It emphasises the importance of continuous learning, personal growth, and tackling new challenges that contribute to both individual and organisational success. In such environments, leadership transcends traditional notions of authority and control. Instead, it is about understanding, listening, nurturing, and developing others. This approach fosters innovation and encourages the cultivation of new leaders who can contribute meaningfully to the organisation's mission.

Within these organisations, every employee, regardless of their formal title or role, has the opportunity to step into a leadership position, all driven by a spirit of collaboration and appreciation. This democratisation of leadership encourages a culture of trust and empowerment, where each individual feels valued and recognised for their unique contributions. As we've discussed before, it is essential to recognise that leadership is not a solitary endeavour. To become a strong, effective, and inspiring leader, collaboration is absolutely essential.

Defining the boundaries of your leadership influence is a crucial aspect of this collaborative journey; you must effectively communicate where your presence and support can be found within the organisation. While you may excel at addressing every aspect of your business and possess a diverse set of skills, attempting to do everything alone can significantly hinder your company's growth and innovation. Instead, by involving others in your vision, empowering them to lead, and fostering an inclusive atmosphere, you can embrace new challenges while conserving valuable time and energy.

This leads us to a pressing question that every leader must consider: who should be entrusted with leadership responsibilities within the organisation? Identifying the right individuals to take on leadership roles is critical for maintaining momentum and ensuring the organisation remains aligned with its vision. This selection process should involve careful consideration of each individual's strengths, values, and potential for growth. By doing so, you cultivate a network of capable leaders who are not only committed to the organisation's objectives but are also inspired to create a positive and impactful workplace culture.

It's often said, 'Power corrupts, and absolute power corrupts absolutely.'

We frequently hear that the pursuit of power or status can lead to one's downfall. However, it's not the 'power' associated with a position that is inherently negative; rather, it's the revelation of character that power brings. It lays bare our true selves, exposing the vulnerabilities and sensitivities we harbour. We grapple with greed, malice, and ambition, often becoming defensive when our egos are challenged. In our quest for validation, we can become so consumed by our selfishness that we lose sight of our responsibilities and the ethical obligations tied to our positions.

When power is within our grasp, there is a risk of misusing it to fulfil our personal agendas, neglecting the duties that come with leadership. To foster a healthy and productive environment, we must be vigilant, ensuring that our leadership serves the greater good rather than personal gain.

A person's life can often be overshadowed by frustrations from the past, feelings of inferiority, and unrealistic fantasies about the future. Their minds become entangled in the ego shaped by their experiences, positions, prestige, and achievements. They reassure themselves of their worth, convincing themselves that they are no less than anyone else. However, in a world brimming with possibilities, abilities, and potential, encountering someone who appears superior or inferior can trigger a need to prove their own superiority. Unfortunately, the mind often resorts to a singular method of asserting dominance: by perceiving others as inferior. It craves authority, power, and recognition, which is why maintaining balance and control over these desires is crucial.

Once you've experienced hardship, attaining a position of power can ignite a desire to accumulate wealth and demonstrate status to those who once overlooked you. If you've faced opposition, the temptation to suppress dissenters can be compelling upon gaining authority. Many are drawn to positions of power because they bring an illusion of superiority, allowing them to act freely without accountability. As a result, individuals cling to their positions, fearing that losing their title would erase their legacy and significance.

However, it's essential to understand that your reputation is rooted in your abilities and character, not merely the title you hold. You have earned your place at the table because of your inherent worth, not the other way around. To truly command respect, focus on those qualities that enrich your character. Wealth, status, and prestige will naturally follow when you cultivate your inner virtues.

Entrusting leadership to someone is a complex and significant responsibility. Your workplace may be filled with talented writers, designers, developers, and marketers, but expertise alone does not equate to effective leadership. Leadership is fundamentally about influencing and motivating others to work together toward a common goal. It requires you to connect with people, understand their value, provide direction, continuously learn, solve problems, and most importantly, take responsibility for the outcomes—not merely seek a title or promotion.

Delegating leadership or creating a leader involves transferring power, which can profoundly affect your organisation and its employees. Therefore, it is imperative to exercise caution when selecting leaders at any level. A poor leader typically prioritises personal interests above all else, while a good leader places the welfare of others before their own. However, this trait alone does not suffice; we must also identify the qualities that can be nurtured and evaluated to develop a capable leader for the future.

Dedication to Purpose and Goals

The essence of leadership lies in guiding individuals within an organisation to collaboratively pursue shared objectives and goals. A person who is truly dedicated to the company's mission and values—prioritising them above personal interests—can be instrumental in leadership roles. Such a leader effectively unites the efforts of others, creating a cohesive environment aimed at achieving success. In reality, commitment to purpose and meaning is synonymous with dedication; it embodies faith and serves as a pathway to success. No significant goal can be realised without a deep sense of dedication. When we approach any task with commitment, we inevitably yield positive outcomes.

Dedication fosters self-discipline, a crucial attribute that keeps you focused on your objectives. It enhances your drive and passion, immersing you fully in your tasks and allowing you to see nothing beyond your goals. This unwavering focus enables better decision-making and propels you forward. A profound sense of dedication is vital for building a successful organisation. It is essential to recognise that dedication is a spiritual quality that cannot be externally imposed; it is an intrinsic feeling. Therefore, cultivating a spiritual workspace culture and inspiring others to share this sense of purpose is imperative for achieving lasting success.

Proactiveness: The Key to Staying Ahead in Life

'Great leaders never act in haste. They remain composed, concentrating on what they can control.'

Regardless of our intelligence, maturity, wisdom, or wealth, we all encounter challenges. As business leaders, we face difficult situations daily. Turning our backs on them or running away is not an option. However, our responses to these challenges are often shaped by our commitment to proactive leadership. In today's fast-paced world, being proactive is essential for success. A proactive leader learns from the past while moving confidently toward the future.

They anticipate challenges and, most importantly, develop strategies to address potential problems.

A truly effective leader does not rush into decisions; instead, they advance with a clear vision for the future. They understand that time is not a luxury they can afford, nor should their reactions be dictated by external circumstances beyond their control. Proactiveness empowers us to concentrate on the elements within our grasp. To effectively tackle any issue, it is crucial to recognise what lies within our control and what does not. Ultimately, what depends on us includes our emotions, decisions, creativity, attitudes, perspectives, ambitions, and determination.

'If you want to find a genuine solution to a problem, focus on its roots rather than merely addressing the surface.'

The primary responsibility of any leader is to actively seek solutions. To do this effectively, it is essential to understand the underlying causes of the problem. As leaders, we cannot depend on luck to resolve issues. Remember, a problem remains unresolved until you take ownership of how it impacts you and consider what you can do differently. You must continually affirm, 'This is my problem, and it is my responsibility to solve it.' This mindset fosters an empowering approach to leadership, enabling you to anticipate challenges, proactively address problems, and guide your company and team toward success, ultimately achieving remarkable outcomes.

Time Management: The Art of Prioritising Tasks

'The ability to prioritise tasks is a fundamental skill that distinguishes great leaders from the rest.'

In today's rapidly changing world, leadership has become increasingly complex. As business leaders, we often juggle multiple projects simultaneously, making efficient time management crucial. Time management is essentially the skill of prioritising tasks—focusing on what truly matters.

We understand that a leader's life is not merely a series of tasks to be completed; it is replete with a multitude of responsibilities that encompass various dimensions of management and influence. A leader's role includes overseeing complex plans, making pivotal policy decisions, coaching team members, solving intricate problems, and inspiring those around them. This multifaceted existence often resembles a train on a journey, racing past numerous stations along its route, pausing only briefly at designated platforms before continuing its relentless march toward its ultimate destination.

Effective time management is not just about being busy; it requires us to thoughtfully determine where to stop along the way, for how long we should linger at each stop, and how we can maintain momentum to keep moving steadily toward our goals. Just as a train conductor must decide which stations to prioritise based on the overall journey, a leader must assess the critical points in their day-to-day operations that warrant attention and focus.

As leaders, mastering the art of prioritising tasks based on urgency and importance is vital. We must identify which tasks are essential for achieving our objectives. Effective prioritisation enables us to allocate resources efficiently, manage risks, and lead by example.

Effective Communication: The Key to Exceptional Leadership

Communication is a fundamental skill for effective leadership. A great leader excels in communication, inspiring and empowering those around them. The success of any leadership is evident in the efficiency of teamwork; it can be measured by how swiftly and seamlessly a team completes its tasks. Strong communication skills are pivotal in achieving these objectives, as they unite team members toward common goals while clearly defining roles and responsibilities. This fosters trust and collaboration.

Effective communication is an essential skill that enables leaders to articulate and convey the team's objectives clearly and effectively, while also fostering an understanding of the aspirations, concerns, and needs of their team members. It serves as a bridge between leadership and the team, promoting an open dialogue that encourages transparency and mutual respect. This open line of communication cultivates a positive rapport between leaders and their teams, which, in turn, enhances overall productivity and efficiency within the workplace. Consequently, it becomes abundantly clear that the mastery of effective communication skills is not just important but absolutely vital in the realm of leadership. The ability to communicate effectively can significantly influence a leader's success in guiding their team toward achieving common goals while ensuring that each member feels heard and valued.

Ultimately, if your actions inspire others to dream more, engage fully, learn, act, and strive for improvement, you are on the path to becoming a successful business leader. A true leader has the ability to influence the personal development of others through extraordinary leadership, shaping them into future leaders themselves.

In reflecting on life, we see each moment slipping away. Despite our desires, we find ourselves inching closer to our final days, yet we remain lost in the pursuit of our ambitions. What is this relentless race about? What truly fulfils our existence? What can we earn that remains with us beyond life itself? In truth, we often spend our lives tallying what we have gained and lost, what we have acquired and relinquished. However, the reality is that all we possess will remain here, and what we create will also be left behind. Throughout our lives, we strive to appear astute at every turn, but what do we ultimately achieve? The sobering answer is often nothing.

It is important to recognise that success in life is transient. What you attain today may take on a different form tomorrow. Therefore, it is futile to equate success with fame, wealth, position, or prestige.

In truth, if there is anything worth earning in life, it is the wealth that lies within. This inner wealth encompasses your meditation, consciousness, spontaneity, awareness, discipline, and resilience. When you cultivate this internal wealth, external accolades—wealth, status, prestige—will follow as a natural gift. Achieving this inner abundance allows you to perceive business and life from a different perspective. You will no longer find yourself running aimlessly in the outside world; instead, your focus will shift inward. Your pace, direction, and partnerships will all originate from within. A traveller on this path feels no sense of being lost. Once your sense of partnership becomes internal, you rise above the relentless pursuit of profit and loss, liberating yourself from the confines of success and failure.

Ultimately, you must strive to attain this internal wealth. If you fail to do so, *'Your company is going to shut down.'*

Companies That Have Thrived for Centuries

1. **Kongo Gumi (578, Japan)**: Renowned for constructing Japan's oldest temples, Kongo Gumi was founded by Shigechi Kongo and specialises in building Buddhist temples.
2. **Nishiyama Onsen Keiunkan (705, Japan)**: Established by Fujiwara Mahito, this hotel has been continuously operated by the same family since its founding, making it a testament to enduring hospitality.
3. **St. Peter Stiftskulinarium (803, Austria)**: Situated within St. Peter's Abbey, this restaurant boasts a history that dates back to 803 AD, earning it the title of the oldest restaurant in the world.
4. **Sean's Bar (900, Ireland)**: Established in 900 AD, this bar is celebrated for its historical significance and charming, ancient atmosphere.
5. **Weihenstephan Brewery (1040, Germany)**: This brewery, originating from a Bavarian monastery, holds the distinction of being the oldest brewery in the world, still operating today.
6. **Munke Mølle (1135, Denmark)**: Located in Odense, Denmark, this flour mill has been in operation since its founding in 1135 AD.

7. **Cambridge University Press (1534, UK)**: Founded by the University of Cambridge, it is recognised as the oldest publishing house in the world.
8. **Beretta (1526, Italy)**: Founded by the Beretta family, this company is celebrated as the oldest firearms manufacturer in the world.
9. **Shumiya Shinbutsuguten (1024, Japan)**: This company specialises in the production of religious robes and items, with a legacy that began in 1024 AD.
10. **Tassel (1548, Belgium)**: Established in Belgium, this brewery ranks among the oldest in the world.
11. **Kremnica Mint (1328, Slovakia)**: Founded in 1328 AD, this minting factory continues to produce coins to this day.
12. **Barovier & Toso (1295, Italy)**: This glassmaking company, founded in 1295 AD in Murano, Italy, remains a renowned producer of specialty glassware.
13. **Royal Delft (1653, Netherlands)**: Founded in 1653, Royal Delft is a manufacturer of traditional Dutch pottery, still thriving today.
14. **F. lli Piacenza (1733, Italy)**: This Italian wool mill, established in 1733, is known for its high-quality woollen products.
15. **Lloyd's of London (1688, UK)**: Originating in a coffee house in 1688, this insurance marketplace is now one of the world's leading insurance markets.
16. **Swarovski (1895, Austria)**: Founded by Daniel Swarovski, this company is renowned for its exquisite crystal products.
17. **Veuve Clicquot (1772, France)**: Founded by Philippe Clicquot, this champagne house is celebrated for its premium champagne offerings.

18. **Antinori (1385, Italy)**: This historic winery, established in 1385, remains family operated and is known for its exceptional wines.
19. **Roku Gin (1658, Japan)**: Founded in 1658, this distillery is recognised as Japan's oldest gin manufacturer.
20. **Tanqueray (1830, UK)**: Established in 1830 by Charles Tanqueray, this gin distillery is known for its high-quality spirits.
21. **Moët & Chandon (1743, France)**: Founded by Claude Moët, this company is one of the most prestigious champagne producers in the world.
22. **Twinings (1706, UK)**: Founded by Thomas Twining in 1706, this tea company is renowned for its premium tea selection.
23. **Kikkoman (1917, Japan)**: Established in 1917, this soy sauce manufacturer is celebrated for its quality products.
24. **Lalique (1888, France)**: Founded by René Lalique, this company specialises in crystal and jewellery manufacturing.
25. **Saint-Gobain (1665, France)**: Founded during the reign of King Louis XIV, this company is known for its high-quality glass production.
26. **Colman's (1814, UK)**: Established in 1814, this spice and sauce manufacturer is famous for its mustard.
27. **Jim Beam (1795, USA)**: Founded in 1795, the Jim Beam distillery is recognised as the oldest bourbon distillery in the world.
28. **Bacardi (1862, Cuba)**: Founded by Facundo Bacardi in 1862, this rum distillery remains family run and renowned for its quality.

29. **Erdinger (1886, Germany)**: Established in 1886, this brewery is one of the oldest wheat beer manufacturers globally.
30. **Ballantine's (1827, UK)**: Founded by George Ballantyne, this company is among the oldest Scotch whisky manufacturers.
31. **Boehringer Ingelheim (1885, Germany)**: Founded by Albert Boehringer in 1885, this pharmaceutical company remains family operated.
32. **Merck Group (1668, Germany)**: Established in 1668 in Darmstadt, Germany, this company is the oldest pharmaceutical and chemical manufacturer in the world.
33. **SmithKline Beecham (1830, UK)**: Founded in 1830, this pharmaceutical company is known for its high-quality medications.
34. **GKN (1759, UK)**: This engineering company, founded in 1759, manufactures products across various industries.
35. **Kraft Heinz (1869, USA)**: Founded in 1869 by Henry Heinz, this food company is famous for its diverse range of food products.
36. **Nestlé (1867, Switzerland)**: Established in 1867 by Henry Nestlé, this food and beverage company is one of the largest in the world.
37. **PepsiCo (1898, USA)**: Invented by Caleb Bradham in 1898, Pepsi was later established as a company, becoming one of the most recognised beverage brands globally.
38. **Unilever (1929, UK)**: Founded in 1929, Unilever is a multinational company renowned for its diverse range of consumer products in the food and beverage sector.

39. **Procter & Gamble (1837, USA)**: Established in 1837 by William Procter and James Gamble, this company began by producing soap and candles and has grown into one of the world's largest consumer goods companies.

40. **Colgate-Palmolive (1806, USA)**: Started by William Colgate in 1806 as a soap and candle factory in New York, the company later expanded into toothpaste and various other consumer products.

41. **General Electric (1892, USA)**: Formed from the merger of Thomas Edison's Edison General Electric Company, General Electric specialises in electrical and lighting equipment, playing a crucial role in technological innovation.

42. **Siemens (1847, Germany)**: Founded by Werner von Siemens and Johann Georg Halske in 1847, Siemens specialises in electrical engineering and electronics, significantly impacting global technology.

43. **Toshiba (1875, Japan)**: Established in 1875 by Tanaka Hisashige, Toshiba is recognised for its manufacturing of electrical equipment and electronics, contributing to advancements in various technologies.

44. **Philips (1891, Netherlands)**: Founded in 1891 by Gerard Philips and his father Frederik, Philips is famous for its lighting solutions and electronic equipment, pioneering innovations in these fields.

45. **Nokia (1865, Finland)**: Originating as a lumber mill in 1865 under Frederik Idestam, Nokia transitioned into a major player in telecommunications and mobile phone manufacturing.

46. **IBM (1911, USA)**: Founded by Charles Ranlitt Flint in 1911 as the Computing-Tabulating-Recording

Company, it evolved into International Business
Machines (IBM) and is a leader in computer hardware
and software.

47. **Coca-Cola (1892, USA)**: Invented by John Pemberton
    in 1886, Coca-Cola was established as a company by
    Asa Candler in 1892 and has since become one of the
    most iconic beverage brands worldwide.

48. **Ford Motor Company (1903, USA)**: Founded by Henry
    Ford in 1903, this company revolutionised automobile
    manufacturing and remains one of the world's leading
    car manufacturers.

49. **Peugeot (1810, France)**: Established as a family mill
    in 1810, Peugeot evolved into a significant player in
    automobile and bicycle manufacturing, known for its
    innovation and quality.

50. **Toyota (1937, Japan)**: Founded in 1937 by Kiichiro
    Toyoda, Toyota has grown to become one of the largest
    automobile manufacturers in the world, renowned for
    its commitment to quality and innovation.

These companies have not only survived the test of time
but have also established themselves as leaders in their
respective industries, gaining worldwide recognition for
their quality, innovation, and consistent performance.
Their longevity speaks to their ability to adapt and thrive
in an ever-changing global market.

www.ingramcontent.com/pod-product-compliance
Lightning Source LLC
Chambersburg PA
CBHW021935190326
41519CB00009B/1028